WALTER

THE ILLUSTRATED STORY OF A RANGERS LEGEND

BY LINDSAY HERRON

PHOTOGRAPHY EDITOR - AILEEN WILSON

OFFICIAL PUBLICATION

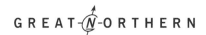

Great Northern Books

PO Box 213, Ilkley, LS29 9WS

www.greatnorthernbooks.co.uk

ISBN: 978 1 905080 540

Original design concepts by The Kemsley Group

Layout: David Burrill

CIP Data

A catalogue for this book is available from the British Library

ACKNOWLEDGEMENTS

I would like to thank Walter Smith for his terrific co-operation not just with this book but throughout his second spell as Rangers manager when, despite enormous weekly demands, he always gave time to the Rangers Media department and always spoke with depth and consideration. It has been a pleasure and a privilege to work with him. Considerable thanks are also due to Natalie Houston who worked tirelessly in the organisation, marketing and promotion of this book.

Lindsay Herron

CONTENTS

INTRODUCTION

WALTER SMITH is arguably the greatest Rangers manager of all time and his achievements at Ibrox undoubtedly make him one of the most successful bosses in world football.

A born and bred Rangers supporter who used to travel from his home in Carmyle in Glasgow's East End to follow the team, he lived the ultimate dream.

In his first spell as manager between 1991 and 1998 he led the Light Blues to a remarkable haul of 13 major trophies which included the Treble, the Double twice and, of course, nine in a row.

He also came agonisingly close to reaching the inaugural Champions League final in 1993 after a fantastic 10-game unbeaten run only to be pipped by one point by eventual winners Olympique Marseille who were subsequently prevented from defending their title after a corruption scandal.

For many Rangers supporters it is the greatest period in the club's history which featured some of the greatest players to ever pull on a blue jersey like Richard Gough, Ally McCoist, Ian Durrant, Mark Hateley, Andy Goram and of course the mercurial talents of Brian Laudrup and Paul Gascoigne.

Rangers dominated the domestic scene with unrelenting power even if the final season of that first spell ended in deep disappointment when Rangers failed to clinch a record 10th successive league title and lost out in the Scottish Cup final.

You have to go back to the 1930s to find a similarly dominant period when Rangers won seven Championships and five Scottish Cups.

Of course, he was also at the heart of all of the successes between 1986 and 1991 when he worked as assistant to Graeme Souness and helped reawaken a sleeping giant to make Rangers the best team in the land. In this period Rangers won three Championships and the League Cup four times and they revolutionised the game in this country for evermore with the change in players' contracts and the calibre of player they lured to Ibrox.

It was the end of an era when Smith left in the summer of 1998 as the majority of his stalwart players left at the same time. It had been announced at the Annual General Meeting that he would be stepping down and it was subsequently announced that Dutchman Dick Advocaat would take over.

Smith took up a post in the English Premier League with Everton, taking trusty lieutenant Archie Knox with him, but it was a tempestuous four years as he had to deal with a very difficult financial period and was constantly forced to sell his best players.

He was sacked by Bill Kenwright in 2002 and it was undoubtedly a low point in his career but he answered the call from the SFA in January 2005 after the ill-fated Berti Vogts era and revitalised the Scottish national team.

However, two years later the lure of returning to Rangers was too strong. The appointment of Paul Le Guen as manager in the summer of 2006 simply did not work out and Smith was brought back to salvage the situation. The litany of success thereafter is extraordinary.

Indeed there are those who feel that Smith's second spell as Rangers manager is actually more impressive than his first given the resources he had to work with and the circumstances within which he found himself working.

He brought Ally McCoist with him from the Scotland set-up to be his assistant and pinched Kenny McDowall from Celtic where he had been working successfully as reserve and youth coach.

He immediately signed Davie Weir, Ugo Ehiogu and Kevin Thomson and steadied the ship in the second half of the 2006/07 season achieving second place in the SPL ahead of Hearts to secure a route into the Champions League.

The following season was one of the most remarkable in Rangers' history. The squad was shaken up as Lee McCulloch, Steven Naismith, Steven Whittaker, Carlos Cuellar, Daniel Cousin, DaMarcus Beasley and Jean-Claude Darcheville - among others - were all signed. They were joined by Steven

Davis, on loan from Fulham, and Neil Alexander and Christian Dailly in the January.

Rangers embarked on a remarkable 18-game European run which led them to the UEFA Cup final where they lost to Zenit St Petersburg in Manchester. They won the League Cup on penalties against Dundee United and then edged out Queen of the South in the Scottish Cup final.

However, horrific fixture congestion cost them their dream of winning the SPL title as Rangers had to play 17 high profile matches in 54 days at the business end of the season.

Undaunted, Smith brought back Kenny Miller to Rangers which was a bold move given that he had played for great rivals Celtic and indeed scored against the Light Blues but he was to prove to be an overwhelming success.

Davis was signed permanently while Kyle Lafferty, Maurice Edu, Pedro Mendes and Madjid Bougherra were also captured. The title was won on the final day of the 2008/09 season and then Rangers completed the Double by beating Falkirk in the Scottish Cup final.

Rangers retained the Championship with some ease in 2009/10 even though they were unable to sign any players and they famously won the League Cup against St Mirren despite having only nine men.

Smith had planned to leave that summer but was persuaded to remain in charge and brought more glory to the club with £4million signing Nikica Jelavic winning a thrilling League Cup final against Celtic.

He then followed that with a sensational final day SPL triumph at Kilmarnock to claim the Championship for a third successive year and his 10th title as manager before handing over the reins to Ally McCoist.

Statistically Bill Struth is the most successful Rangers manager with 30 major trophies in his 34 years but it is plain to see why many feel Walter Smith is simply the best.

Lindsay Herron

BY SIR ALEX FERGUSON

THERE can be few men in world football who have achieved so much and delivered such wonderful success to one club than Walter Smith.

His glories with Rangers are utterly exceptional and, in my view, are unlikely to be repeated. But that does not tell the whole story.

The success he brought to Rangers in the 1990s was fantastic. He carried on the great work that he had started with Graeme Souness and, of course, won nine successive League Championships.

For that alone he would be worthy of being classed as one of the great Scottish managers because it equalled the feat set by Jock Stein at Celtic two decades earlier.

However, he came back to Rangers for a second time and for me the success he brought in that period was quite ridiculous. He hardly had any money to work with and yet he made Rangers multiple winners again and not only that, led them to a European final.

Getting to the UEFA Cup final in 2008 was quite staggering actually because all or most of their victories were achieved away from home.

Rangers seemed to play the first leg at Ibrox and achieve a goalless draw and then do the job away. It was fantastic. So it was one of the great achievements.

I went to the final and I took my grandson Jake with me. I thought Rangers did really well in the first half but then they had a penalty claim turned down when Barry Ferguson had a shot blocked by the arm.

You just felt it drained away after that. If they had got the lead they would have had a great chance. They would have been very difficult to beat.

I have known Walter since the early 1970s although I am sure we came up against each other in a few reserve matches when I was still with Rangers in the late 1960s so the link goes back even further.

He was always interested in the coaching side of the game and I knew he was progressing very well in that regard at Dundee United.

When I went to Aberdeen in 1978 I felt he would be ideal to have as my assistant.

I was on holiday in Malta at that time. In fact, I will never forget it because it was the day of the World Cup final between Argentina and Holland.

I called Jim McLean to ask permission to speak to Walter and you could hear his response back in Scotland!

He screamed at me 'He's got a six-year contract and a four-year option'. Poor Walter was one of those belt and braces, chained to the wall contracts that wee Jim specialised in.

He was threatening all kinds of legal action against me and was just short of sending the mafia round! He was not too pleased.

So I then had to explain to Walter that it wasn't going to happen.

Jim McLean had him on a player contract and that was the real problem. If Walter had been on a coach's contract then he could have walked away but he had a good relationship with Dundee United and whether he would have done that I'm not sure. It certainly would have been a difficult decision.

So I was knocked back and I took Pat Stanton with me to Pittodrie and then Archie Knox came on board after that.

Of course at this time a great rivalry was beginning between Aberdeen and Dundee United and because of that Jim and Walter and myself and Archie became close.

I got to know Walter well and when I took over the Scotland job when Jock Stein sadly passed away I made Walter my assistant with the national team.

By that time Walter was getting respected as one of the top coaches in the country and that's one of the main reasons I took him with me as my assistant at Scotland.

I was then offered the Arsenal job in early 1986 and again I wanted to take Walter with me. I thought I would sound him out when we were on Scotland duty together. We were going to play in Israel and I didn't know that Walter was going to Rangers at that time.

So while we were in Tel Aviv I told him that I had been offered the chance to go to Arsenal and I asked him what he thought.

He was positive about it, saying they were a big club and that kind of thing. So I said to him 'Do you fancy coming with me?'

Then he dropped the bombshell that he was going to Rangers. I said 'when did this happen?' and he told me it was a long story but he would fill me in later.

Of course I later learned that Graeme Souness had been lined up to take over and Walter was going to Ibrox with him.

The thing about the Arsenal offer was that they wanted an answer right away but I couldn't give them one because I was going to the World Cup in Mexico with Scotland.

So the Arsenal thing fell by the wayside. Walter went to Rangers and then later that year I went to Manchester United.

Walter was the ideal man for Graeme because Graeme had no idea about Scottish football for a start. All of his life had been in England after going to Tottenham as a 15-year-old and then to Middlesbrough and on to Liverpool.

We were reunited in 2004 at Manchester United because I needed someone to assist me in the run-in that season and I knew Walter was the man for the job.

Carlos Quieroz was coming back that summer and Walter knew it would be a short-term thing but he was delighted because he wanted to work. He did a smashing job, the players loved him and we won the FA Cup that year.

It's been a pleasure to have worked with him and it's been a bigger pleasure to know him.

CHAPTER ONE

REALISING THE DREAM (1986-91)

WALTER SMITH realised the boyhood dream of signing for Rangers when he became an integral part of the Graeme Souness Revolution on April 7, 1986 just 29 months after he thought his only chance had come and gone.

Smith was assistant manager at Dundee United to Jim McLean where they had achieved terrific success topped by the winning of the Scottish Premier Division Championship in 1983.

That autumn McLean was approached to become Rangers manager following the resignation of John Greig after Alex Ferguson had rebuffed Rangers' advances and he would have taken Smith with him had he accepted. He refused and Smith was shattered.

However, the call came again less than three years later and this time Smith could make his own decision. Revolution was in the air at Ibrox and Smith as assistant manager was to be a major part of the new dawn.

He said: "One of the reasons Graeme brought me on-board was because he didn't know much about Scottish football.

"I had knowledge of the players and the set-up so I was able to help him in that way.

"However, the whole impact that it had and everything that happened in the coming years was all down to Graeme – he was the catalyst."

Smith had grown up a Rangers supporter in Carmyle in Glasgow's East End. He followed the team whenever he could, regularly travelling on the local supporters' club bus.

So he, more than anyone, was acutely aware of how much the lack of success in the early 1980s had hurt the supporters.

Rangers were in a poor state at the time. They had not won the Championship since 1978 and the Scottish Cup had not been lifted since 1981.

They scraped into Europe on the final day of the 1985/86 season and then the fun really began.

Smith said: "It was a fantastic time to be involved with Rangers. The whole of the close season was unbelievable as we made the build-up to the new season.

"It is undoubtedly one of the highlights of my career, simply being in at the beginning of it all and being part of it at that time."

The fans craved information on who Souness and Smith were going to bring in and it was the shattering of the Ibrox wage structure which paved the way.

Smith said: "Rangers had the traditional thing where players were paid the same money, but that changed right away.

"The whole thing was gathering momentum and the shocks kept coming.

"We brought the captain of England to Rangers. The fact that Terry Butcher came to Rangers ahead of a number of top English clubs was a fantastic thing.

"We also signed Chris Woods and brought in Jimmy Nicholl a little bit later on and the whole thing was snowballing, but we actually did not make that many changes in that first season.

THE TOP TEAM ... Walter Smith was appointed assistant manager when Graeme Souness was sensationally named as boss on April 7, 1986 and the two men set about reawakening a sleeping giant.

LEFT:
WELCOME ABOARD ....
David Holmes, the Rangers chairman at the
time, was the man behind the audacious move
to capture Graeme Souness as manager and his
first "signing" was Walter Smith.

ABOVE: DOWN TO BUSINESS ...
Souness and Smith made massive changes in the
early days. Striker Colin West (centre) was the
first new face when he joined from Watford but
the signings that shocked the football world
were England captain Terry Butcher, who arrived
from Ipswich for £725,000, and England
goalkeeper Chris Woods, who was captured from
Norwich for £600,000.

"There was also a great reaction from the existing players. We had guys like Ally
McCoist, Ian Durrant and Derek Ferguson while Davie Cooper had a fantastic
season."

It all started in a blaze of controversy, however, when the player-manager
Souness was sent off in the first league game of the season against Hibs at
Easter Road for kicking George McCluskey.

It sparked a melee in the centre circle involving all 22 players – apart from
Hibs' goalkeeper that day Alan Rough. Rangers lost the match 2-1 and the press
naturally had a field day.

However, from that inauspicious start a bond seemed to develop within the
dressing room and the results began to come.

There is little doubt that the League Cup final on October 26, 1986 was a huge
catalyst for Souness and Smith.

It was a gripping Old Firm occasion played in front of 74,219. Durrant gave Rangers the lead with a cool left-footed finish only for Brian McClair to equalise for Celtic from the edge of the box.

Then with six minutes remaining, Roy Aitken pulled down Terry Butcher at the back post and referee Davie Syme pointed to the spot. The Rangers fans behind Pat Bonner's goal held their breath but they need not have worried as Cooper dispatched the perfect spot kick to win the trophy.

In the league from November 29 until April 4 Rangers went on a 19-game unbeaten run. Finally, a nine-year wait was over at Pittodrie on May 2, 1987 but the match with Aberdeen was not without its controversy.

Souness was sent off again but with 10 men Rangers battled on manfully. Perhaps appropriately it was the new captain Butcher who headed Cooper's inch-perfect free kick into the net and although Brian Irvine equalised Celtic's 2-1 home defeat by Falkirk meant that Rangers were the champions for the first time since 1978.

Smith said: "It was just an incredible year. To win the title was massive and it was the perfect start for all of us."

Souness and Smith were knocked back on their heels in the 1987/88 season to a certain degree as Celtic came back strongly under the returning Billy McNeill.

However they suffered badly from suspensions and injuries, most notably to Terry Butcher who broke his leg against Aberdeen on November 17 and did not play again that season.

The League Cup was retained in a fantastic final with Aberdeen on October 25 when the two sides finished level at 3-3 after extra time and Rangers won on penalties with Durrant scoring the decisive kick.

However, the Championship went back to Parkhead. Indeed Rangers finished third in the table behind Hearts who claimed the runners-up spot.

On the positive side Richard Gough was signed while Mark Walters, Ian Ferguson and John Brown were all brought on-board and all four were to become hugely significant figures in the years ahead.

Souness introduced many new things to Rangers and one of them was to take the team to a pre-season training camp at Il Ciocco in the Tuscany hills. It was there that much of the conditioning and preparations were made.

The team was evolving all the time with players like Dave McPherson and Robert Fleck being sold and others like Colin West, Neil Woods, Mark Falco and Trevor Francis moving back to England.

Graham Roberts, a vital man in the early days having joined from Tottenham for £450,000, also left in controversial circumstances when he fell out with Souness but Rangers made a £25,000 profit when the sold him to Chelsea for £475,000 in August 1988.

ON TOP OF THE WORLD ... Captain Butcher carries Ian Durrant on his shoulders as they celebrate the fantastic League Cup win over Celtic on October 26, 1986 which gave the new management team the perfect start at Ibrox.

THE GOAL THAT WON THE TITLE ... Ally McCoist races to celebrate with Butcher after his bullet header at Pittodrie on May 2, 1987 clinched the Premier Division title giving Rangers the Championship for the first time in nine years.

On the plus side Gary Stevens arrived from Everton for £1million and he was joined by striker Kevin Drinkell from Norwich City for half of that amount.

Rangers were fresh, strong and organised when they began the 1988/89 campaign. They didn't know it then but the odyssey which would lead them to nine Championships in a row began at the old Douglas Park, Hamilton with a 2-0 win over the Accies.

Celtic were hammered 5-1 on a gloriously sunny day on August 27 which still lives long in the memory for many Rangers fans who especially savour the stunning volley from Ray Wilkins.

The League Cup was won for a third successive season on October 23 and again it was a classic final with Aberdeen. It was on a knife-edge at 2-2 when Ally McCoist settled it from inside the six-yard box.

There was one notable absentee that day – Ian Durrant. The hugely talented midfielder had been cut down in his prime by a shocking and savage challenge by Neil Simpson in a 2-1 defeat at Pittodrie 15 days earlier.

Durrant's knee was in tatters and he was out of action for two and a half years. He bravely returned and became a highly effective player for Rangers, with his skills, passing and penchant for scoring vital goals.

However, he was never quite the same player as that dashing youthful talent that broke through under Jock Wallace and then flourished under Souness and Smith.

Of course, 1988 was the year that Rangers changed ownership when David Murray, encouraged by Souness, bought over the majority share-holding of the club for £6million from Lawrence Marlborough, so ending a long family dynasty at the club.

The young self-made millionaire bought into the Souness-Smith era at Rangers literally and metaphorically and for the next decade an almost unparalleled level of success and glory was achieved.

Celtic were hammered again at New Year, this time 4-1, and in a powerful second half to the season Rangers were crowned champions when Drinkell and Mel Sterland both scored doubles in a 4-0 win over Hearts.

LEFT: CHAMPIONS AT LAST ... Rangers were presented with the Championship trophy on May 9, 1987 after the final match of the season – a 1-0 win over St Mirren – with Smith beside Souness, hidden by Derek Ferguson.

.

RIGHT: NEW METHODS, NEW SUCCESS, NEW PLAYERS ... Souness changed the pre-season plans at Rangers by taking the squad to a specialised training camp in Italy at Il Ciocco. The Light Blues retained the League Cup in 1987/88 with an epic penalty shoot-out win over Aberdeen after a 3-3 draw. And they plundered England again in 1988 bringing Kevin Drinkell from Norwich for £500,000 and Gary Stevens from Everton for £1million.

HERE'S TO THE CHAMPIONS ... Walter Smith raises his glass as Rangers celebrate bringing the title back to Ibrox in 1989 following a 4-0 victory over Hearts. Little did anyone know it was the beginning of an unbelievable stranglehold of the crown.

FANTASTIC TIMES ... David Murray took ownership of Rangers in October 1988 when he concluded a deal with Lawrence Marlborough and had the drive and ambition to take Rangers to even greater heights. The title was retained in 1990 and Butcher celebrated in style at Tannadice after a Trevor Steven goal secured more success.

Suddenly the Treble was in Rangers' sights but they were denied a clean sweep by Celtic when Stevens was short with a pass back and Joe Miller nipped in to score the only goal of the game.

That was a watershed moment, not because Rangers had failed to win all the major honours but because Celtic would not win a trophy again for six years.

Souness, of course, was never a man who was far from controversy and he made the boldest move possible in the summer of 1989 when he usurped Celtic and made the first major Catholic signing in nearly 50 years when he brought Maurice Johnston to Rangers.

It was a sensational story, especially as Johnston had previously played for Celtic, and it shook Smith to the core that Souness had the bravery to see it through.

It proved to be a masterstroke. Mo finished top scorer that season and scored against his old team twice, most notably a last minute winner on November 4, 1989 at Ibrox which secured his hero status with the Rangers legions.

The signing of Johnston from Nantes seemed to crush Celtic, who had paraded him as the returning prodigal son ahead of the 1989 Cup final only for Souness to pull off the signing coup of the century.

Trevor Steven had cost as much as Johnston - £1.5million from Everton – but he seemed to slip in under the radar and the other key capture that season was Nigel Spackman who offered more combative strength than silky Wilkins who

returned south to Queen's Park Rangers.

Aberdeen and Hearts were Rangers' closest challengers that season with Celtic finishing a distant fifth. It was Steven who clinched the title with a header at Tannadice on April 21.

Still the big names came to Ibrox as Souness splashed out £1million for Mark Hateley from Monaco and spent even more on Oleg Kuznetsov but the Soviet international suffered major knee damage almost immediately.

Terry Butcher was sensationally sent to Coventry – quite literally – after a fall-out with Souness ahead of the League Cup semi-final with Aberdeen in September and so Richard Gough captained the side in the final against Celtic on October 28.

It proved to be a momentous occasion as it was Gough who ventured forward to score the winning goal in extra time as Rangers triumphed 2-1. It also proved to be Rangers' last major honour under Souness.

Increasingly frustrated by the Scottish football authorities and the effect his high profile in Scotland was having on his private life, when the Liverpool job became available he was ready to accept.

And so it came to pass that despite David Murray's protestations Souness left Rangers for Anfield on April 16, 1991 with just four games left in the chase for three titles in a row. All of a sudden the door flew wide open for Walter Smith.

MO-MENTOUS ... Souness and Smith stunned the world when they signed Mo Johnston from under the noses of Celtic so the striker was hardly given a warm reception when he played at Parkhead on August 26, 1989. The capture seemed to crush Celtic's spirit as Rangers romped to more glory.

LEFT: WE'VE DONE IT AGAIN ... Rangers celebrate the Championship triumph of 1990 when they were presented with the trophy on April 28 after a 2-0 win over Dunfermline.

HAPPY DAYS ... Souness holds the Championship trophy aloft after a cameo appearance against Dunfermline.

THE BACKROOM TEAM ... Physiotherapist Phil Boersma, Doctor Donald Cruickshank, Graeme Souness and Walter Smith.

LEADING THE WAY ... Walter Smith gets his point across at training.

COUPLE OF SWELLS ... Smith and Souness delivered so much success together.

SOUR AND SWEET ... Terry Butcher was literally sent to Coventry when he fell out with Souness but the glory kept coming. Richard Gough skippered Rangers to a dramatic extra time League Cup win over Celtic scoring the winning goal after Mark Walters had scored earlier.

WHAT A SHOCKER ... David Murray announces to a packed media conference that Graeme Souness is to leave Rangers to become manager of Liverpool.

CHAPTER TWO

INTO THE HOT SEAT (1991/92)

IT was on April 17, 1991 that Walter Smith was announced as only the ninth man to become manager of Rangers and it was undoubtedly the proudest moment of his life.

But suddenly he had a Championship to win and it took a monumental feat in a final day shoot-out with Aberdeen.

Graeme Souness had asked Smith to go with him to Liverpool but Walter resisted the temptation, hoping that he would win the opportunity to take over at Rangers but he faced an anxious wait.

Smith said: "Graeme asked me to go to Liverpool but when I looked at the staff down there everyone was in place and I couldn't see a position for me.

"I will always be grateful to Graeme for taking me to Rangers and for the great five years we had together.

"David Murray called me and asked me to take the team for the rest of the season. He then told me a couple of days later that I was in his thoughts to take over and that was a big thing because Rangers were in a position to attract any number of established managers.

"Then he met me at Ibrox before our next game away to St Mirren and he offered me the job which was fantastic. He asked me to keep it quiet for a week – and I still don't know why – and then I was announced as the new manager which was undoubtedly the proudest moment of my career."

He immediately brought in as his assistant close friend and former Dundee United team mate Archie Knox, who gave up a plum role with Sir Alex Ferguson at Old Trafford and the prospect of the European Cup Winners' Cup final against Barcelona in Rotterdam which Manchester United duly won.

Intriguingly, Rangers were offering Knox more money than he was on at Old Trafford and the Manchester United board refused to up the ante. It was a sign of how powerful Rangers were at this time.

Smith said: "We had always stayed in touch, phoning each other every week. He had been a manager in his own right and highly successful as an assistant to Fergie at Aberdeen and Man United so securing his help was vital."

Suddenly Rangers had four games left to win the Championship – the third in succession – but a disastrous 3-0 defeat at Motherwell in their penultimate match put Aberdeen in the driving seat.

The Dons came to Ibrox on May 11 needing a draw to win the title on goal difference. On one of the most remarkable days in the club's history Rangers beat them 2-0, despite being ravaged by injuries before and during the game.

Mark Hateley still had some detractors following his signing the previous summer but his towering header from Mark Walters' cross and then a simple tap-in after Michael Watt fumbled Mo Johnston's shot elevated him to hero status.

In the most demanding of circumstances the Championship was theirs. It was a massive moment for Smith in the very early days of his reign and it was a sign of things to come.

Having kept hold of the crown he set about making his own mark on the squad although there was a sense of necessity about it as a new UEFA ruling meant that each team was only allowed to field three non-nationals in European competition.

It meant that Englishmen were classed as "foreigners" and

MY PROUDEST MOMENT .... Walter Smith realised the ultimate dream when he was unveiled as Rangers manager by David Murray on April 17, 1991 to replace Graeme Souness who had left for Liverpool.

WELCOME WALTER ... The football world waited and wondered what Rangers would do after Graeme Souness left the club but Walter Smith was the obvious choice to replace him and he was introduced at a press conference beside captain Richard Gough. His first "signing" was to appoint long-time friend Archie Knox (bottom left) as his assistant.

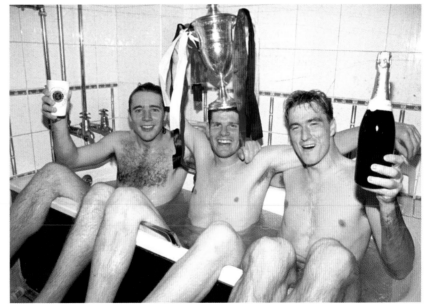

SENSATIONAL ... Mark Hateley roars in celebration after his stunning header gave Rangers the lead in the game that won the Championship. He scored a second goal to clinch a memorable win.

OFF AND RUNNING ... Walter Smith gleefully holds aloft the Championship trophy after winning the title in the Ibrox decider with Aberdeen.

TOP MARK ... Hateley salutes the adoring Ibrox fans after one of the most amazing and important Championship successes in Rangers' history.

GAME FOR A BATH .... Ally McCoist, Ian Durrant and Ian Ferguson knew there was only one way to celebrate the Championship success!

Smith had to be watchful of that aspect as he made his moves into the market.

To that end Chris Woods was sold to Sheffield Wednesday and Mark Walters went to Liverpool while Trevor Steven was transferred to Marseille for a then club record of £5.5million. Mo Johnston also left, joining Everton.

In came Andy Goram from Hibs, David Robertson from Aberdeen, Stuart McCall from Everton and the mercurial Alexei Mikhailichenko from Sampdoria in Italy. All proved to be terrific players for Rangers in the years ahead.

Smith said: "We had to face the prospect of the three foreigners rule but in a way it was the best thing that happened to us as it freshened things up.

"I actually didn't want to make too many changes. I knew it would take a little time for the team to gel and so it proved but once it did they played some great stuff.

"We lost out in Europe to Sparta Prague early on and then went out of the League Cup but experience has taught me that it takes time for new players to settle and in the end we managed with a League and Cup double."

The elevation of Smith to manager proved to be a godsend for Ally McCoist who began to form a devastating partnership with Hateley which plundered 56 goals that season.

The team really kicked into gear over the winter months and Rangers went on a 16-match unbeaten run between

DEADLY ... Scottish defences failed to cope with the pace and power of Mark Hateley in Smith's
first season in charge.

WHAT A DOUBLE ACT ... Hateley and McCoist were a joy to behold as Rangers romped to a
League and Cup Double.

WE'VE DONE IT ... John Brown celebrates with Walter Smith after the dramatic Scottish Cup
semi-final victory over Celtic.

ALLY BE PRAISED ... Scottish Cup semi-final goal hero McCoist celebrates with first team coach
Davie Dodds.

IT'S FOUR IN A ROW ... The Rangers players and management celebrate after romping to the title with a 4-0 win over St Mirren at Ibrox.

FANTASTIC START ... Walter Smith celebrates the Championship with skipper Richard Gough (above) and poses with the old trophy with assistant boss Archie Knox.

November 30, 1991 to March 14, 1992 which included 14 wins and the squad was bolstered by the signings of winger Dale Gordon from Norwich and striker Paul Rideout from Notts County.

They saw off Hearts by nine points winning the Championship with a 4-0 win over St Mirren on the 18th of April. Re-born striker Ally McCoist scored two of the goals and overall claimed 39 that season.

The Scottish Cup had proved elusive during Smith's five-year partnership with Souness but he won it in his first season. Indeed it was on a torrential night at Hampden on March 31 in the semi-final against Celtic that Smith's new team really showed its mettle.

Remarkably Rangers saw off the challenge of their great rivals despite playing for 84 minutes with only 10 men after Robertson was sent off for a reckless challenge on Joe Miller.

Showing remarkable resilience Rangers produced a 1-0 victory with McCoist taking a pass from McCall and memorably thumping a low shot into the left corner at the Rangers End of Hampden.

It was 11 years since Rangers had won the Cup – a 4-1 replay win over Dundee United in 1981 when Smith was assistant to Jim McLean at Tannadice – so the pressure was on to finally bring the old trophy back.

Lying in wait were Airdrie who were bossed by 1970s Rangers star Alex MacDonald; one of the members of the iconic team that won the European Cup Winners' Cup in Barcelona on May 24, 1972. It turned into a glory day for the Light Blues with McCoist and Hateley both scoring.

Smith said: "The semi-final was a key moment for us because it cemented the unity of the team. We lost Davie Robertson early in the game to a red card and we were up against it against a good Celtic team but we came through to win 1-0 with an Ally McCoist goal.

"That result as much as anything showed the spirit and determination of the new group.

"We then beat Airdrie in the final 2-1 with Hateley and McCoist scoring and it was fantastic to finish the season with the Double."

OUR CUP RUNNETH OVER ... Walter Smith celebrated his first full season in charge by clinching the Double when Airdrie were beaten 2-1 in the Scottish Cup final with Mark Hateley and Ally McCoist scoring the goals. He made it a family affair by sharing the joy with his wife Ethel and sons Neil and Steven (right).

CHAPTER THREE

THE TREBLE AND EURO GLORY (1992/93)

RANGERS have enjoyed some incredible campaigns in their long and illustrious history but it is hard to find many – if any – to match the remarkable efforts of Walter Smith's side in 1992/93.

It was an epic season full of drama, quality, glory and guts with a tinge of sadness and regret thrown into the mix.

Rangers swept the boards on the domestic scene for the first time in 15 years and for only the fifth time in their history and it was Aberdeen who suffered as a result.

The Dons were beaten in both cup finals and they were the nearest challengers in the Premier Division, which was then a gruelling 44-game campaign.

It was only the second time in the club's history that the Championship had been won for five successive seasons some 62 years after Bill Struth's dominant force achieved this highly impressive feat.

In Europe Rangers were electrifying. They qualified for the inaugural Champions League – a competition originally devised by Rangers director-secretary Campbell Ogilvie – in the most stunning and memorable way when English champions Leeds United were beaten home and away.

They came within an ace of reaching the final in Munich. Instead Marseille won through to play AC Milan and triumphed with Basile Boli's goal separating the sides. They were, however, prevented from defending the trophy by UEFA amid sordid revelations of corruption in France which led to them being relegated and heavily fined.

The club's owner Bernard Tapie was imprisoned for his involvement and there were always suspicions and rumours about Marseille's European run that season.

Ally McCoist won the prestigious Golden Boot for finishing top scorer in Europe that season – even though he broke his leg playing for Scotland in Portugal a month before the end – while Andy Goram was voted Scotland's Player of the Year.

It was the zenith of Walter Smith's first period in charge of Rangers and it remains one of the greatest achievements of any team.

It was largely achieved with the same group of players that had delivered the Double the previous year but there were some key additions.

Dave McPherson, who had been sold to Hearts in 1987 for £325,000, was brought back for £1.3million and played 53 matches in all competitions. He had developed into an influential defender and had played well for Scotland at the Euro 92 Championships in Sweden.

Ironically Trevor Steven returned from Marseille as the French club had defaulted on transfer payments and also played a key role while Ally Maxwell arrived from Motherwell for £300,000 as back-up to Goram and played 10 times in the league.

Out went Paul Rideout to Everton while Nigel Spackman and

WE'VE SWEPT THE BOARDS .... Walter Smith and his trusty assistant Archie Knox proudly pose with the League Cup, the Scottish Cup and the League Championship trophy after Rangers won the Treble for the fifth time in their history.

young striker John Spencer were sold to Chelsea for a combined total of just under £1million.

Smith said: "It was a fantastic achievement by the team that year.

"The whole season was exceptional. You could see that the team was getting a togetherness that was to stand us in good stead."

Rangers made a decent start to the season beating St Johnstone and Airdrie and then being held to a goalless draw at Easter Road against Hibs.

They then suffered a surprise defeat at Dundee, who had just come up from the First Division, and some questions were asked. No one knew at the time but it was a watershed moment.

Smith said: "We started the season reasonably well and then lost 4-3 to Dundee at Dens Park.

"It was a strange game because we played very well that day but every time Dundee went up the park they scored.

"From that point on we went on a run of 44 matches without losing a game which was quite remarkable when you consider it also included matches against our European opponents that season – Marseille, Bruges and CSKA Moscow.

"We had some good luck at that time but we also played particularly well and to go on such a run without defeat is a terrific achievement."

Ian Durrant, always the man for the big occasion, secured a 1-1 draw at Parkhead in the first Old Firm game of the season and then Aberdeen were beaten 3-1 at Ibrox with

Durrant scoring the first goal and setting up McCoist perfectly for the second.

Rangers were now off and running and they won their next 10 matches to show that they meant business in the defence of the Championship.

McCoist scored an astonishing 16 goals in this explosive run of victories which also included a vital Parkhead win over Celtic on November 7 when Durrant proved to be the match-winner after McCoist set him up.

By this point Rangers had already secured the first major trophy of the season when they defeated Aberdeen in the League Cup final on October 25, 1992.

It was a strange day in many ways and a very tight match which went into extra time. Rangers took the lead in unusual circumstances and from an unusual source.

The new back pass rule had just come in where goalkeepers could not pick the ball up and when David Winnie knocked the ball back to Theo Snelders he chested it into the path of Stuart McCall who gleefully tucked the ball into the net.

Duncan Shearer produced an equaliser when he swivelled on the edge of the box and shot past Andy Goram but Rangers won it in added time when Gary Smith inadvertently headed Davie Robertson's cross into his own net.

The final came four days after the first leg with Leeds United at Ibrox and the two matches with the English champions are occasions that Smith will never forget.

Rangers had comfortably knocked out Danish title winners Lyngby in the preliminary round, winning 2-0 at Ibrox through Mark Hateley and Pieter Huistra and then 1-0 in Copenhagen when that man Durrant notched another vital goal.

WELCOME BACK ... Trevor Steven returned to Rangers when Marseille defaulted on transfer payments while Dave McPherson was bought back from Hearts. Both were key men in an epic season.

It set up a meeting with Leeds, then bossed by Howard Wilkinson, and no one in England gave Rangers a chance. Smith had other ideas but he could hardly have got off to a worse start.

Gary McAllister stunned and silenced the Ibrox crowd in the first minute when he produced a stunning volley from the edge of the box from Gordon Strachan's corner which ripped into the top left corner of the net.

This Rangers team was made of strong stuff, however, and their recovery was aided by some eccentric goalkeeping by John Lukic who punched the ball into his own net from Ian Durrant's corner.

Then the master goalscorer secured a 2-1 win. Lukic couldn't deal with Dave McPherson's header and Ally McCoist swept the rebound into the net.

Even then the English media were still writing off Rangers. They were convinced the champions of England would be too strong in the second leg. They could not have been more wrong.

Like the first leg there was an early goal but this time it was Rangers who scored it. Elland Road was stunned when Mark Hateley let fly with a powerful looping volley which flew over Lukic and into the net.

Then in a stunning, sweeping move Durrant sent Hateley charging down the left wing and he crossed to the back post where McCoist dived to head into the net. Eric Cantona pulled one back for Leeds but Rangers had sent them tumbling out.

Smith said: "The matches with Leeds were fantastic. They were a good side at the time and they had not been beaten at Elland Road for a long time so to win both matches against them was terrific and something I never really expected to do.

"Of course it was billed as The Battle of Britain and it was pleasing to show our English colleagues that we could muster up a good enough team."

The Rangers players and management stayed in Manchester that night and there was some serious partying going on. Indeed when Walter Smith came down to breakfast the following morning he found Stuart McCall

DANISH SIZZLERS .... Pieter Huistra (above) and Mark Hateley (middle) put Lyngby to the sword in the first leg of the Champions League preliminary round at Ibrox in a 2-0 victory and then Ian Durrant notched the vital away goal in Copenhagen to take Rangers through to face Leeds United with some ease.

BEST OF BRITISH ... Stuart McCall and Mark Hateley (top) celebrate after the stunning opening goal at Elland Road in the Battle of Britain. Ian Ferguson and Richard Gough dominate Lee Chapman in the air at Ibrox (middle) and Ally McCoist scores with a brilliant diving header after a majestic sweeping move.

SUITS YOU SIRS .... Walter Smith and his Rangers players are looking sharp in their club suits as they celebrate the League Cup success over Aberdeen on October 24, 1992 when the Dons were beaten 2-1 at Hampden.

SKOL RIGHT NOW ... Stuart McCall (above) was a goal hero for Rangers in the League Cup final – then sponsored by Skol Lager – and the victory sparked great celebrations for the Rangers players at Hampden after the extra-time win over Aberdeen.

HEAD MAN ... Mark Hateley was a massive figure in the group opener against Marseille and famously scored with a diving header to earn Rangers a thoroughly deserved point against the French champions.

EURO HEROES ... Rangers secured a vital away win over CSKA Moscow in a match played in Bochum, Germany when Ian Ferguson's shot was deflected into the net and then Pieter Huistra was on target in Belgium in a 1-1 draw with Bruges.

and first team coach Davie Dodds sitting in the foyer with pints of beer and large cigars.

When Smith suggested that the lads should maybe get their act together and start thinking about their next match McCall replied: "Don't worry gaffer, it's only Celtic." Rangers promptly won that Old Firm game on November 7 as mentioned earlier in this chapter.

It was an indication of the tremendous spirit and togetherness that exuded from this special group of players who certainly knew how to celebrate their successes but undoubtedly went about their work in some style.

Rangers moved into the group phase and they opened up at Ibrox against Marseille. On a muddy night Rangers found themselves two down after Alen Boksic scored from close range and then German striker Rudi Voller capitalised on a slip by young defender Steven Pressley.

However, they mounted a sensational comeback with substitute Gary McSwegan looping a header into the net and then Hateley diving to nod in an equaliser. Indeed such was the momentum of the team they might well have won that game but the French side held out.

Next up were CSKA Moscow away but because of the severe Russian winter the December 9 match was played in the German city of Bochum. It was almost like a home game for Walter Smith's side because 90 per cent of the 9000 crowd were Rangers fans and Ian Ferguson's deflected shot gave them a 1-0 win.

Dutch winger Pieter Huistra earned Rangers a vital 1-1 draw in Bruges and then Rangers defeated the Belgians 2-1 at Ibrox with Durrant scoring a terrific goal and Scott Nisbet netting with one of the most bizarre goals ever seen at Ibrox.

His attempted ball into the box took a wicked deflection, bounced in front of bemused keeper Dany Verlinden and over his head into the net. Ibrox erupted with joy but the victory came at a huge cost as Hateley was sent off for raising his arms and was suspended for the two remaining matches.

Rangers then went to southern France on April 7, 1993 knowing that if they beat Marseille they would qualify for the Champions League final. They went behind to a Franck Sauzee goal and then Durrant scored a magnificent, swerving equaliser.

It finished 1-1 and qualification was out of Rangers' hands. They went into the final game against CSKA Moscow level on points with Marseille but the French side were eight goals better off in terms of goal difference.

Raymond Goethals' side beat Bruges 1-0 in Belgium and it made Rangers' goalless draw with the Russians irrelevant although there was no hiding the disappointment of the players as they trooped from the field.

Smith said: "Overall the European run was marvellous. We were unbeaten in our four qualifying matches and then we were unbeaten in all of our group matches, just missing out on the European Cup final itself."

Rangers consoled themselves with the prospect of winning

BLUE AND WHITE DYNAMITE ... Rangers were sensational at home against Bruges when Ian Durrant (top) drove in a fantastic right foot shot and then Scott Nisbet (bottom) scored with a quite freakish effort which took a wicked deflection and bounced over keeper Dany Verlinden to keep the Champions League final dream alive.

SO CLOSE TO GLORY ... Rangers needed a win in Marseille to reach the final and were then helpless in their final game against CSKA Moscow. The line-up that night was: (back) Richard Gough, Davie Robertson, Dave McPherson, John Brown, Ian Durrant, Pieter Huistra; (front) Andy Goram, Trevor Steven, Stuart McCall, Ian Ferguson, Ally McCoist.

FIVE IN A ROW ... the Championship was clinched at Airdrie when Gary McSwegan's goal took Rangers over the line. Stuart McCall and Dale Gordon and Davie Robertson got into the party spirit at Broomfield while injured Ally McCoist gave the Ibrox fans a laugh by wearing an Oliver Reed cut-out on his back before joining his team mates for the official presentation.

ABOVE: TREBLE YELL ... an amazing season was topped by the Scottish Cup final win over Aberdeen. Richard Gough lifted the trophy to spark the celebrations after Mark Hateley and Neil Murray (bottom left) scored the goals that gave Rangers a 2-1 win over the Dons to seal victory. For Walter Smith (above right) it was an historic moment.

LEFT: THREE AND EASY ...the victorious Rangers players celebrate the Scottish Cup which gave them the Treble and, of course, it was all the sweeter because the final with Aberdeen took place at Celtic Park.

the Championship on the 1st of May at Broomfield and they duly completed the mission with Gary McSwegan scoring the only goal against Airdrie.

The title was won without McCoist who sadly broke his leg in Lisbon's Stadium of Light as Scotland crashed to a 5-0 defeat to Portugal on April 28.

Now a clean sweep was on and it was Aberdeen who stood between Rangers and the Treble in the Scottish Cup final on May 29 and the prospect was further enhanced by the fact that the showdown was to take place at Celtic Park because of renovations to Hampden.

Rangers were not going to let the opportunity pass them by and despite one of the most arduous seasons in living memory they responded one more time when it mattered.

Those who thought that Rangers had nothing left in the tank were proved very wrong.

Once again Hateley was devastating as he raced forward to smash a left foot shot into the net and then Rangers scored a second goal when Neil Murray's shot was deflected past Theo Snelders.

Lee Richardson made it a tense finish with a terrific right foot strike but Rangers held on to win and secure the grand slam of Scottish football.

The Dons had pushed Rangers all the way that season but within 20 months their manager Willie Miller was fired.

Smith said: "Sometimes luck plays a big part and there are occasions when you are simply unlucky.

"For Willie Miller to be the manager of Aberdeen at the time when Rangers were having such great success must rankle with him.

"He led Aberdeen into two finals against Rangers and lost them both and then finished runners-up in the league to us.

"However, he was working in an environment at Aberdeen where the incredibly successful Sir Alex Ferguson period was still fresh in the minds of the people there.

"I have no doubt that Rangers' successes that season cost Willie his job in the end and you have to say that it was harsh treatment.

"From our point of view we had a season that few teams have ever had and one we will always remember.

"The players were exceptional that year, continually producing big performances when we needed them."

It was undoubtedly a season that Walter Smith will never forget.

BOARD APPROVAL .... the 1992/93 season will live long in the memory as one of the greatest in Rangers' history. The board of directors (from left) Campbell Ogilvie, Ian Skelly, chairman David Murray, vice chairman Donald Findlay and Jack Gillespie celebrated the achievement with Walter Smith in the Blue Room at Ibrox.

CHAPTER FOUR

DOMINANCE AND SUPERSTARS (1993-96)

THE ARDUOUS task of improving upon the near perfect season was virtually impossible but Walter Smith came mightily close to emulating it and then in the following two seasons set about bringing players to Rangers that the fans could only previously dream about.

Smith almost led Rangers to the unprecedented feat of winning the Treble in consecutive seasons and then he stunned the football world by firstly signing Brian Laudrup from Fiorentina in the summer of 1994 and then Paul Gascoigne from Lazio a year later.

All the while the major silverware continued to be housed in the Ibrox trophy room and the fans had never had it so good.

Smith said: "We had a base of a team that was very successful in that period. We won seven trophies in a row. We were going for the first ever double treble but lost the 1994 Cup final to Dundee United.

"I think three years of football at a high level takes its toll on players and we needed a bit of freshness and we certainly got that from Brian Laudrup initially and then Paul Gascoigne a year later.

"The team needed a bit of a spark and both players brought that to us. Both were individually brilliant players and they changed the way we set up.

"Previously we were more of a unit and they were individuals so it was a little bit difficult to fit them into a team but both were capable of winning a game at any time.

"That was the problem they posed to any opposition because in an instant they could turn a match."

In the summer of 1993 Smith smashed the Scottish transfer record by signing Duncan Ferguson from Dundee United for £4million but for reasons beyond his control it proved to be a short-lived experience.

Ferguson, a boyhood Rangers fan whose hero had been Davie Cooper, ended up being sentenced to three months in jail for head-butting John McStay of Raith Rovers during a league match at Ibrox on April 1994.

He was an Everton player by the time he served his sentence in Glasgow's Barlinnie Prison, initially moving to Goodison on loan and then completing a move which cost £4.2million.

One of the reasons he had been brought in was due to Ally McCoist's convalescence from a broken leg suffered in April 1993 but his success at Rangers was limited.

Indeed it was the man many felt would be affected most by his arrival, Mark Hateley, who was the catalyst to Rangers' success in the league Championship that season

Hateley picked up the mantle to inspire those around him and scored 22 league goals in a season when Rangers were most forcibly challenged by Aberdeen and Motherwell.

The season, however, started in a nightmarish fashion. Having scaled the heights of Europe the previous season and holding aspirations of reaching the summit they were

SILVER LINING .... the signings of Brian Laudrup and Paul Gascoigne took Rangers to a new level and the two of them were at the heart of the many successes in the mid—1990s including the sensational 5-1 Scottish Cup mauling of Hearts when Gordon Durie scored a hat-trick.

GLORY DAYS .... the jubilant Rangers players celebrate the fantastic League Cup final success of 1993 made famous by Ally McCoist's match-winning overhead kick.

GATHERING MOMENTUM ... Walter Smith paid a club record £4million to Dundee United for striker Duncan Ferguson in the summer of 1993. In November he spent £1.2million to capture Gordon Durie from Tottenham and he played a major part in the glories ahead. The League Cup success was a sixth consecutive trophy for Smith and assistant Archie Knox and a special guest appeared at the celebrations in the shape of legendary 1920s and 1930s striker Bob McPhail.

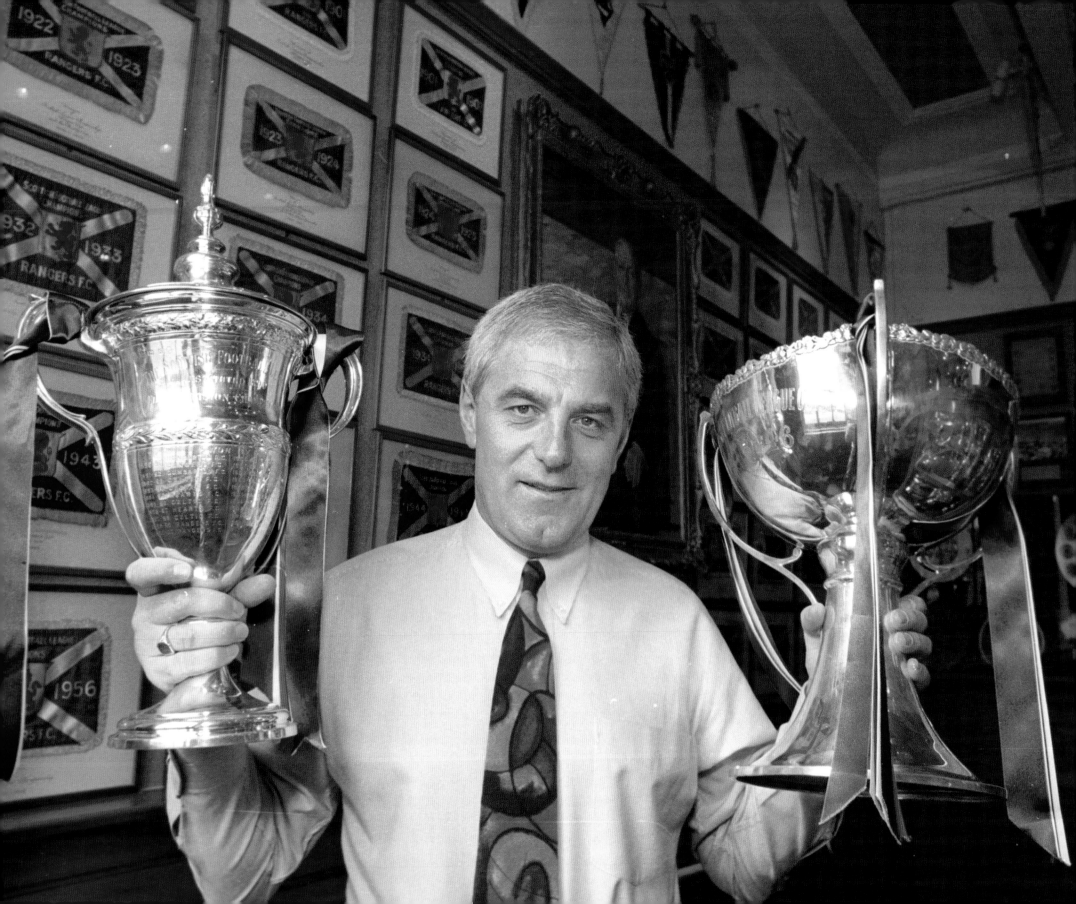

crudely brought back down to earth in the Bulgarian capital of Sofia.

Rangers held a 3-2 lead over Levski when they travelled east. They were tied at 1-1 with just seconds remaining after Ian Durrant had scored a priceless away goal. They were dreaming of another exciting campaign in the Champions League but it was ripped from them when Nikolai Todorov smashed a shot high over Ally Maxwell and into the net.

It was a killer blow but the perfect tonic came a month later in the League Cup final on October 24 when returning hero Ally McCoist produced a script that Roy Race would have been proud of.

Rangers had reached the final by beating Celtic 1-0 – again against the odds when Pieter Huistra was sent off for stupidly kicking out at Tom Boyd. Durrant robbed Mike Galloway on the right and drove a low cross into the box which was swept into the net by Hateley.

Rangers were up against Hibs and the match was finely poised at 1-1 after Durrant had scored with an exquisite lob and Dave McPherson had unfortunately put the ball into his own net.

Time for the fairytale to unfold. Nowhere near fit, McCoist was summoned from the bench and it was one of those remarkable moments when he reacted to a long throw-in and produced a stunning overhead kick which tore past Jim Leighton.

Durrant couldn't believe his eyes. He said with a grin after the game: "He's stolen my thunder again but we'll go off and blow the froth off a few and reminisce!"

Curiously the beer was not touched when Rangers actually won the Championship on the 3rd of May, 1994. A crate had been left for them in the dressing room at Easter Road but they lost 1-0 to Hibs and only landed the title due to results elsewhere.

Remarkably the Light Blues won only half of their 44 league fixtures that season and flat is the best way to describe the way they finished the season. They failed to win any of their remaining five fixtures and that was hardly the way to go into the Scottish Cup final looking

LEFT: TWO GOOD ... Walter Smith proudly displays the League Championship trophy and the League Cup after another terrific campaign in 1993/94.

SIX IN A ROW ... the title was Rangers' again in 1994 and the players revelled in their latest glory. First team coach Davie Dodds joined in as did Walter's father Jack (middle right picture, centre) and club doctor Donald Cruickshank. Ally McCoist cracked open the bubbly with Trevor Steven but the campaign ended in disappointment for captain Richard Gough and his players when Dundee United beat Rangers 1-0 in the Scottish Cup final to stop unprecedented back to back Trebles.

to make history.

Smith recalled: "We definitely had a problem that season at the end. I think the fatigue of playing so well and in so many huge matches the previous season had taken its toll."

Dundee United stood between Rangers and the grand slam for a second successive season and the goal that won it for United was tragi-comic. Dave McPherson was short with a back pass, Ally Maxwell panicked and kicked the ball straight at Christian Dailly whose shot from a tight angle hit the post and rolled along the line giving Craig Brewster the easiest tap-in of his life.

It was time to freshen things up. Smith had sent his trusty lieutenant Archie Knox to go and watch Denmark in action with a view to making a move for Michael Laudrup which seemed audacious to say the least given that he was playing with Barcelona at the time.

Knox obviously knew of his brother Brian's qualities and it became clear that Rangers might be able to get him as he had become disillusioned with life in Italy where he played with Fiorentina and also AC Milan on loan.

The stunning deal which cost £2.2million was done in the summer of 1994 and those who watched Laudrup in the ensuing seasons feel privileged. He had a devastating effect on the Scottish game.

Smith, of course, has scarcely worked with anyone better but, intriguingly, he feels Laudrup should have been even better.

He said: "Brian Laudrup is as good a player as I have ever worked with but he frustrated me a little.

"He had the capability of being up there with the greatest players of all time; there is no doubt about that.

"There was just that little bit in him mentally that maybe stopped him from being right at the very top.

"Make no mistake he was a fantastic player for us, but I felt he could have elevated himself into a position where he was one of the best in the world.

"He was a great, great player for Rangers and a really great guy."

RIGHT: WHAT A DEAL ... Rangers fans could hardly believe it when David Murray and Walter Smith clinched a deal to bring Laudrup to Ibrox.

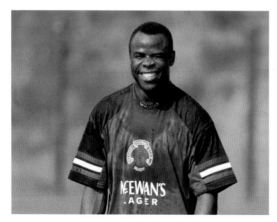

A NEW LEVEL .... Walter Smith showed he meant business when he signed Brian Laudrup from Fiorentina and the great Dane made a sensational impact and loved his first Old Firm goal in a 3-1 win on October, 1994. Basile Boli and Alan McLaren were also recruited and maybe it was a sign of things to come when Smith chatted with McCoist on the training field.

SEVENTH HEAVEN .... Walter Smith, Archie Knox and all of the Rangers players revelled in a seventh successive Scottish League crown in a season dominated largely by the skills of Brian Laudrup.

Laudrup undoubtedly lit up Rangers in the 1994/95 season and the Light Blues ended up winning their seventh consecutive title with some ease, finishing some 15 points ahead of Alex McLeish's Motherwell.

His transfer was actually cheaper than the £2.7million Rangers paid for Basile Boli but their fortunes could hardly have been more contrasting.

Boli had been the lynchpin of the Marseille defence that two seasons earlier had broken Rangers' hearts in the Champions League but he was uncomfortable in Scotland, especially when he had to play at right back on some occasions.

The season had started inauspiciously. Indeed it was crisis time as far as the tabloids were concerned when Rangers were eliminated from the Champions League at the qualifying stage by AEK Athens, lost 2-0 at home to Celtic in the league and were then sent tumbling out of the League Cup at home to Falkirk – all in the space of a week!

Laudrup's mesmeric skill then began to kick in and they were entirely evident when Rangers next met Celtic on October 30, 1994. Celtic were using Hampden as their home while Parkhead was being redeveloped and the Great Dane lit up the national stadium scoring once in a 3-1 win with Hateley netting a double.

By this time Alan McLaren had come on-board with Dave McPherson moving back to Hearts in the deal. Earlier Gary Stevens had left for Tranmere Rovers and the unfortunate Oleg Kuznetsov was allowed to leave for Maccabi Haifa while Steven Pressley was sold to Coventry City for £600,000.

Indeed McLaren's debut came in that October Old Firm win and he only missed two matches for Rangers for the rest of the season. Sadly injuries took their toll on him within four years and in 1999 he was forced to retire at the age of 28.

Alex Cleland came from Dundee United and he was to fit very well into a new system that Smith was crafting for the ensuing campaigns playing in a right wing back role.

Smith, however, shocked the world again in the summer of 1995 when he went back to Italy to sign Paul Gascoigne for

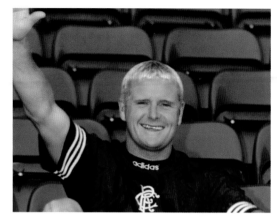

GEORDIE GENIUS ... Smith pulled off another stunning signing coup when he lured Paul Gascoigne from Lazio in the summer of 1995 and the man who wore the No8 shirt promptly delivered Championship No8 in a row with a remarkable hat-trick against Aberdeen. He and Brian Laudrup added flair and imagination to a Rangers side which had been bolstered in January 1995 with the arrival of Alex Cleland.

£4.3million from Lazio.

It was a stunning coup. Everyone knew about Gazza's madcap antics with Newcastle and Tottenham before he went to Italy – and with the England national team.

He had also been troubled by a host of injuries but when he played football there were few to touch him in the world and that was the Gascoigne Smith wanted.

Of course there were explosive headlines at times, but Gascoigne was instrumental in the eighth successive league title.

Smith said: "He was a player you had to get on your side and he also frustrated me as Brian did for different reasons.

"Paul has no attention span whatsoever and it certainly doesn't stretch to 90 minutes.

"At times you would see him wandering around the pitch and then someone would give him a kick up the backside – whether it was me or another player – and you would get an immediate response from him.

"He was an immensely talented player. As Billy Connolly once said, sometimes you have to live with the genius rather than the genius live with you.

"That was Paul Gascoigne. It was a roller-coaster ride but an enjoyable one at that."

Rangers faced a resurgent Celtic that season under Tommy Burns and Gazza hurt them early scoring at half-reconstructed Parkhead in a 2-0 win and he wowed the Rangers fans with his swagger and style.

He also scored 14 goals that season which was a terrific return from a midfield player. However, he saved the best of these for the penultimate league match of the season when he single-handedly won the Championship with a stunning hat-trick against Aberdeen.

He somehow scored from close range from a tight angle but then Brian Irvine equalised for the Dons. Gazza then took the game by the scruff of the neck and from his own half embarked on an amazing run which finished with a cool left foot finish. He finished it all off with a penalty kick.

Smith said: "I don't think there was a better goal than the second goal Gazza scored in the match with Aberdeen which gave us our eighth successive Championship.

"He had scored the first goal in the match and then he produced this remarkable run and tremendous finish to really ease the tension that day.

"Then to get a hat-trick in the game that won us the Championship was terrific.

"That was the type of player he was. If you put him in an environment where he had to go and win something he would always flourish."

Rangers were not finished, of course, as Hearts were to find to their severe discomfort. The 1996 Scottish Cup final will forever be known as the Laudrup Final as he ripped the Tynecastle men apart.

He scored two and set up all three for Gordon Durie who became the first Rangers player to score a hat-trick in this fixture as Rangers won 5-1.

TREBLE YELL ... Paul Gascoigne produced an astonishing performance in the penultimate game of the 1995/96 season when he scored a hat-trick against Aberdeen to win the Championship. Walter Smith reckons his second goal – a solo run from his own half – is probably the best of his Rangers reign.

WE SALUTE YOU ... Archie Knox, Walter Smith, Gazza, Trevor Steven and Davie Dodds play to the jubilant Ibrox crowd after the epic 3-1 win over Aberdeen that clinched the title.

EIGHT IS GREAT .... the Rangers players celebrate the eighth successive
Championship with Gazza deciding to wear the trophy as a hat!

UNSTOPPABLE ... Brian Laudrup produced one of the greatest individual performances ever seen in a Scottish Cup final when he ripped Hearts apart in 1996, scoring two and setting up three for Gordon Durie in the 5-1 hammering

ANOTHER YEAR, ANOTHER DOUBLE ... Gazza congratulates hat-trick hero Gordon Durie while Richard Gough lifts the Scottish Cup to clinch a League and Cup Double. Walter Smith savoured the victory over Hearts and his players lapped up the Hampden atmosphere.

BELL'S® PREMIER DIVISION

WINNERS SEASON 96/97

CHAPTER FIVE

NINE IN A ROW AND FAREWELL
(1996-98)

CHARLIE MILLER hared down the left wing at Tannadice, whipped over a tempting cross and Brian Laudrup came flying through the air to bullet a header into the Dundee United net.

It was a spectacular and special way to finally clinch a ninth successive Championship and ensure that Walter Smith and his players would forever be etched into the history of Scottish football.

An odyssey which had begun on August 13, 1988 at the old Douglas Park in Hamilton ended on May 7, 1997 at the home of Dundee United and it sparked scenes of unbridled joy.

Remarkably, a year later Smith and the bulk of his nine in a row heroes had gone and Rangers entered a new phase in their history under Dutchman Dick Advocaat.

The legacy they left behind is huge and, in all probability, their feat is unlikely to be emulated. It is difficult to imagine another nine in a row, but you never know!

Of course Jock Stein's Celtic had achieved nine successive titles first between 1966 and 1974 and the pressure on Smith and his squad to equal this was utterly intense when the 1996/97 season got underway.

Indeed the pressure was just as intense on the Parkhead club who were desperate to stop Rangers from reaching their objective and, as mentioned in the last chapter, they were a far more formidable force under Tommy Burns than they had been earlier in the decade.

Incredibly, Rangers completed the grand slam against Celtic that season winning all four league fixtures and that undoubtedly contributed massively to the extraordinary success.

Once again Laudrup was a huge player for the Light Blues, invariably saving his best performances for the matches that mattered. He finished top scorer in the league that season with 16 goals.

Gascoigne also chipped in with 13 league goals despite missing over two months of the season with injury.

Smith said: "You always have to handle the pressure at Rangers but there is no doubt that the nine in a row season was a difficult one to handle.

"Having achieved what we had up until that point we knew that the fans expected us to go all the way and that, of course, was not lost on the players."

Smith made two big summer signings when he spent £4million on Hamburg captain Jorg Albertz and splashed out £2.7million on Swedish international defender Joachim Bjorklund from Italian side Vicenza.

It was a sure sign that the manager meant business and he needed both players from the outset as Alan McLaren was out with a knee problem at the start of the campaign and Davie Robertson was also sidelined forcing Albertz to play at left back.

CLOUD NINE .... the remarkable run of league success culminated in sheer glory at Tannadice on the 7th of May, 1997 with the clinching of 9 in a row and there is no hiding the joy of Walter Smith and his players.

LEFT: COME ON! ... Paul Gascoigne celebrates a stunning breakaway goal against Celtic on September 28, 1996 which clinched a vital 2-0 victory to give Rangers momentum in a momentous campaign.

SPREADING THE NET ... Walter Smith plundered the European market in the summer of 1996 when he signed Jorg Albertz from Hamburg for £4million and then landed Swedish defender Joachim Bjorklund from Italian side Vicenza.

Not many Rangers fans knew much about the flame-haired German but it was not long before he became a firm favourite. In the first Old Firm game of the season on September 26, 1996 he set up both goals in a 2-0 Ibrox win.

Richard Gough rose superbly to power a header into the net from Albertz's out-swinging corner and then he set up peroxide-blonde Gazza to head a second goal when Celtic were ruthlessly taken apart on the break.

It was the seventh consecutive win from the start of the season and clearly signalled Rangers' intent. There were a couple of blips when Rangers lost at Easter Road and were held by Aberdeen at home and then Raith Rovers away but they made their intentions clear again when they beat Celtic 1-0 at Parkhead on November 14 thanks to Laudrup's low drive after Brian O'Neil slipped and gifted possession.

Ten days later the Ibrox Trophy Room was once more graced with the presence of the League Cup after a thrilling final against Hearts at Celtic Park which was

DERBY DAZE .... Danish striker Erik Bo Andersen was the hero for Rangers in the critical New Year derby with Celtic when he scored two late goals to secure a hugely significant 3-1 victory.

HEARTS BREAKERS .... Rangers celebrated a stunning League Cup success over Hearts on November 24, 1996 when two goals each from Paul Gascoigne and Ally McCoist (left) gave them a 4-3 win.

NINE IS SUBLIME ... Brian Laudrup races to celebrate his flying header which clinched 9 in a row and the celebrations started for Ally McCoist, Walter Smith and emotional captain Richard Gough.

WET AND WILD... the heavens opened when Rangers celebrated their fantastic title success back at Ibrox after the final game of the season at Tynecastle but that didn't dampen the spirits of Ally McCoist and Walter Smith who addressed the adoring crowd.

a triumph in particular for Ally McCoist and Gascoigne.

McCoist's record in the tournament is sensational with nine medals to his name and he thoroughly earned this one with two excellent goals to send Rangers clear but just before half-time McCoist slapped Gascoigne on the head for not picking up his man and their on-field row spilled into the dressing room.

In the interim Stevie Fulton had pulled one back and then John Robertson equalised just before the hour mark and suddenly Rangers had a game on their hands. Cue Gascoigne to strut his stuff.

The maverick Geordie had gone into a hospitality suite at half-time and sunk a double whisky and he promptly secured another double with two wonderful solo goals. Davie Weir pulled one back at the death but it was all smiles in the end for Ally and Gazza.

The New Year game with Celtic in the league was another massive moment. Albertz hammered a sensational free kick past Stuart Kerr only for Paolo di Canio to equalise and then Smith sent on Danish striker Erik Bo Andersen who scored twice to send the manager into wild celebrations as he ran down, arms raised in front of the East Enclosure.

Celtic were effectively killed off at Parkhead on March 16 when a patched-up side including emergency loan keeper Andy Dibble and returning Mark Hateley secured a 1-0 win when Durrant's lob was forced over the line by Brian Laudrup.

But Rangers made things hard for themselves when they flopped at home against Motherwell when they had the chance to clinch the crown.

Smith said: "We had managed to get ourselves into a good position; indeed a position where we had three matches left to clinch the Championship and then there was an international break.

"The players all came back on the Friday and as usual that was a bit unsettling and we went into a game at Ibrox against a good Motherwell side and we lost 2-0.

"So then we had to go to Tannadice in the midweek and the lads undoubtedly had a feeling that they had to make up for what had happened on the Saturday and they put in a terrific performance.

"For me that was Brian Laudrup's best game for Rangers – goal aside. He was absolutely terrific that night.

"The whole team dug in. We had one or two injuries but the team responded and it was a tremendous relief when they did it.

"I really did feel the pressure that season, I must say, so it was fantastic to finally win it."

It is one of the great enigmas as to why Rangers did not go on and set a new record with a 10th successive Championship and they had it within their grasp

RAINING CHAMPIONS ... the weather might not have been the best but it could not dilute the fantastic achievement of 9 titles in a row and the players celebrated with the fans at Ibrox holding flags to signify each success.

MADE IN ITALY ... Serie A was plundered by Walter Smith when he signed Sergio Porrini from Juventus, Rino Gattuso and Marco Negri from Perugia and paid Fiorentina nearly £4million to sign Lorenzo Amoruso.

with just four games to go.

Smith signed a new three-year contract in the summer of 1997 and then raided the Italian market in the quest for 10 bringing in vastly experienced defender Sergio Porrini from Juventus for £3million, Fiorentina centre back Lorenzo Amoruso for nearly £4million and striker Marco Negri from Perugia for £3.75million.

In addition he landed terrific Swedish midfielder Jonas Thern from Roma on a free contract and also youngster Rino Gattuso, who was a teammate of Negri's at Perugia.

Unfortunately Amoruso was injured right away and missed virtually all of the season and Smith asked Richard Gough to come back from the United States where he was playing with Kansas City Wiz.

Negri was a sensation in the first half of the season scoring 30 goals by December 27 but Celtic had the edge after a 2-0 New Year win. The pendulum swung in Rangers' favour after they recorded the same scoreline on April 12 but they lost two of their remaining four matches.

It had been announced in October 1997 that Smith was to step down at the end of the season and in February 1998 it was confirmed that Dick Advocaat would be taking over.

Sadly for Smith it was a double disappointment at the end of the season as Rangers then lost the Scottish Cup final 2-1 to Hearts. It was the end of an era as the bulk of the team who played that day left with the departing manager.

He said: "The thing that annoyed me most about that was that we were in a good position to do it.

"We had beaten Celtic near the end of the season and that put us in the driving seat and then managed to lose to Kilmarnock at Ibrox and that effectively cost us 10 in a row.

"No disrespect to Celtic who had shown good consistency throughout the season but we should have been good enough to win that year.

"I had announced that I was to be leaving at the end of the season and a lot of people felt that was one of the reasons we didn't win 10 in a row and if it was, it was.

"From my own point of view, we got very close and we also got the Cup final but unfortunately lost that to Hearts.

"One of the main problems was keeping the team going. We had a lot of players who had been with us for that whole period like McCall, Durrant, McCoist, Gough and Goram.

"They had played a lot of football during that time and it was hard to keep them going to the end.

"A lot of them were leaving that summer – maybe as many as nine or 10 – so I felt that if they were not getting contracts and they were leaving then the time was right for me to do the same.

"It was just really disappointing that it was the only season we didn't win anything."

Smith was quickly re-employed at Everton but his four years at Goodison were difficult in the extreme due to financial restrictions and it was remarkable he avoided relegation.

In 2004 he spent five months with Manchester United assisting Alex Ferguson and, of course, he rejuvenated the Scottish national team during two years in charge. However, in January 2007 the king would return.

TEARS OF JOY ... Ally McCoist is full of emotion after scoring a diving header which clinched victory over Celtic in the Scottish Cup semi-final on April 5, 1998 as Richard Gough and referee Jim McCluskey look on.

CHANGING OF THE GUARD ... it was announced in February 1998 that Dick Advocaat and Bert van Lingen would be replacing Walter Smith and Archie Knox at Ibrox and there was a special testimonial match for the departing manager against Liverpool and a gala dinner at Glasgow's Thistle Hotel.

NEW CHALLENGE ... Smith and Knox were unveiled as the new management team at Everton in the summer of 1998 but it proved to be a difficult period due to the financial restrictions at the club.

CHAPTER SIX

RETURN OF THE KING (2007)

PAUL Le Guen came to Ibrox in the summer of 2006 with a reputation that stretched the length of the Champs Elysees but he lasted barely seven months and holds the unwanted distinction of being the shortest serving Rangers manager.

Everyone had bought into the appointment of the Frenchman as a replacement for Alex McLeish and his CV was mightily impressive having led Olympique Lyon to three consecutive French titles and qualified for the knock-out phase of the Champions League.

However, for a variety of reasons his tenure at Ibrox simply did not work. His team, filled with uninspiring signings, lacked consistency, seemed soft-centred and were well adrift in the title race before Christmas. There was also disharmony in the camp.

It all came to a head at the end of the year when Le Guen stripped Barry Ferguson of the captaincy and dropped him for the Motherwell match on January 2. Le Guen and his backroom team were gone two days later.

Rangers were seemingly in disarray and Chairman Sir David Murray knew there was only one man to come in and retrieve the situation. That man was Walter Smith.

Smith had resurrected the pride and the fortunes of the Scotland team having taken over from Berti Vogts in January 2005 and famously defeated France 1-0 at Hampden in what proved to be his penultimate match in charge.

On January 10 he was officially announced as Rangers manager for a second time.

He said: "I got a phone call out of the blue from Sir David Murray who told me that Paul Le Guen was going to leave and wanted to know if I would be interested in coming back.

"I was rather surprised to say the least. I would never have thought of leaving the Scotland job for any other position especially as we were in the middle of a qualifying campaign.

"It left me in an awkward position and it was a very difficult decision to make but I felt it was an offer I couldn't turn down."

Smith brought with him Ally McCoist, who had been his lieutenant with Scotland, and then pinched Kenny McDowall from rivals Celtic where he had been highly successful with the reserve and youth teams.

He said: "I needed a younger staff and my initial plan was that I would come back for a couple of seasons and help, if I could, settle the place down a bit and then leave and give someone else the opportunity to take over the reins.

"These thoughts were shared with Sir David Murray and we both agreed that Alastair would be the man who would come into that category.

"He had worked with me at the national team and done a very good job so I felt it was only natural that he would come with me back to Rangers.

"He readily agreed and that was one down. Ian Durrant was already at the club as a coach but I still felt I needed to get another one to offer a different perspective.

"Kenny McDowall was someone that many people had spoken about. He had been the reserve coach at Celtic and had done a very good job there so I felt he would be a good addition."

BACK WHERE HE BELONGED ... Walter Smith answered the call to return to Rangers after the ill-fated Paul Le Guen rein and after some haggling with the Scottish Football Association over compensation he was officially unveiled at the Rangers Training Centre on January 10, 2007.

Smith's first task was to steady the ship. The Championship was over and Rangers were out of both cups. He had to secure a place in the qualifying phase of the Champions League for 2007/08 and he knew he needed more muscle.

He said: "Rangers had just lost to Dunfermline in the Scottish Cup and were 17 points behind in the Championship and under threat for second place from Hearts and Aberdeen.

"So it became clear that the first priority was to secure second place and therefore Champions League qualification.

"We set about having a look at the team and we realised that we needed to get a couple of British-type central defenders and managed to get Davie Weir and Ugo Ehiogu and also signed Kevin Thomson from Hibs.

"The first match against Dundee United was a nervous one – even if the 5-0 scoreline does not suggest it – because there was a danger that it would be abandoned at half-time because of the weather.

"It was a great start for us and one I wouldn't have foreseen. From then on we had a good run of wins and later on in the season we managed to secure that second place in the league and therefore qualifiers in the Champions League.

"I obviously used all of these matches to look at the squad and in these circumstances there are players who want to leave and those who want to impress to try to stay."

Two wins against rivals Celtic certainly cheered the fans up. On the 11th of March Smith won his first derby in his second spell when Ehiogu was the unlikely match-winner with a spectacular overhead kick at Parkhead.

It was the first derby win for Rangers in seven matches and they followed it up on the 5th of May when Celtic came to Ibrox, albeit with the Championship already in their possession.

Kris Boyd scored his one and only Old Firm goal while Charlie Adam fooled the Celtic defensive wall and keeper Artur Boruc when hit a free kick under the wall and into the net in a 2-0 victory.

OUT AND IN .... Paul Le Guen left Rangers after only seven months in charge and Walter Smith immediately recruited Ally McCoist and Kenny McDowall to his backroom team.

STRENGHTENING THE SQUAD ... Smith immediately improved the team by bringing in Davie Weir from Everton and paid £2million to Hibs for Kevin Thomson. Smith's first game back was an emphatic 5-0 win over Dundee United on January 13.

BACK IN THE OLD ROUTINE ... Walter took charge of Rangers again for the first time on January 13. Horrific weather threatened to wash out the match but Rangers produced a performance worthy of his return with an emphatic 5-0 victory.

OFF AND RUNNING ... it was Charlie Adam who scored the first goal of Smith's second spell in charge in the 5-0 win over Dundee United and it made the early days back on the training ground all the sweeter for the returning manager.

A SIGN OF THINGS TO COME ... Carlos Cuellar faced Rangers in the UEFA Cup for Osasuna and became one of the major new signings in the summer of 2007.

FIRM INTENTIONS ... Barry Ferguson celebrates the 1-0 victory over Celtic on March 11 with Ugo Ehiogu and Filip Sebo as Walter continued his remarkable record of Old Firm wins in his first derby back.

HERE UGO, HERE UGO, HERE UGO ... Ehiogu was the unlikely match-winner with a spectacular overhead kick in Smith's first Old Firm clash of his second spell. Kenny Miller doesn't look too pleased but he was to have happier days when he returned to Rangers.

These victories certainly helped as Smith settled things down at the club largely using the same players who had effectively lost the title before the end of 2006.

He said: "We enjoyed two Old Firm wins in that first spell and these were obviously very welcome but Celtic were well ahead in the league and we would much rather have been in their position than ours.

"In the Old Firm environment you always want to get a victory over your rivals as quickly as possible and we did that.

"So we finished the season well enough and we knew that the summer would be a very important period for us.

"We knew we would have to reinforce our group in the close season."

It would indeed be a busy summer and one of the major new names was Carlos Cuellar who had played against Rangers in the UEFA Cup in March.

Smith said: "We played against Osasuna and, of course, Carlos Cuellar was in their ranks. We had known about him beforehand because John Brown had gone out and done a bit of scouting for us.

"He told us that they had a few good players and Carlos was one of them. And before the end of the season Martin Bain and myself managed to go out to Madrid and secure his services for the following season and he turned out to be a terrific player for us."

With Champions League football secured Rangers headed to California post-season for a team-bonding trip and a match with LA Galaxy who were preparing for the arrival of David Beckham.

The squad played golf and generally relaxed but plans were already being hatched for the following season as Smith knew the squad had to be strengthened.

They delighted Rangers fans in the area who were treated to a visit from Walter Smith and his squad. The players mingled with the LA True Blues at the local bar where they watch Rangers matches, posed for pictures and signed autographs.

Rangers then faced the Galaxy at the Home Depot Centre and beat them 1-0 with Kris Boyd scoring the only goal on a balmy night in Southern California.

In July the years were rolled back when the 9 in a row heroes reunited for special 10th anniversary celebrations with a challenge match against a Scottish League Select and a gala dinner.

It was an incredible spectacle for the supporters as all of the key men from the fantastic league run between 1988/89 and 1996/97 came back together to celebrate their remarkable achievement.

Brian Laudrup, the man who scored the goal that clinched the ninth title at Tannadice, starred in the match which finished 2-2 and was watched by a crowd of 30,797.

It was a pleasant distraction for Smith but the hard work was just starting.

DERBY DELIGHT ... Charlie Adam celebrates with the Rangers fans after his free kick flew under the Celtic wall to secure a 2-0 Old Firm victory after Kris Boyd had netted earlier in the game on May 5, 2007.

LA STORY .. Rangers headed to Tinseltown at the end of the 2006/07 season for a glamour friendly against LA Galaxy. Walter Smith and Nacho Novo attended a pre-match press conference at the Home Depot Centre along with Frank Yallop and Landon Donovan and then in the match itself Rangers recorded a 1-0 win over the MLS outfit with Kris Boyd scoring the only goal. Charlie Adam is pictured in action with Cobi Jones while Davie Weir marks Donovan.

FRIENDLY FOES ... Walter Smith and Alexei Lalas, then chief executive of Galaxy and former captain of the US national team, exchanged gifts ahead of the challenge match at the Home Depot Centre.

OLD FRIENDS REUNITED ... Rangers celebrated the 10th anniversary of 9 in a row with a special Ibrox challenge match between the title heroes and a Scottish League Select. A crowd of 30,797 watched Rangers draw 2-2 with Brian Laudrup and Pieter Huistra scoring. It was like being back in the old routine for players like Jorg Albertz and Richard Gough and the fans saluted their heroes at the end.

CHAPTER SEVEN

AN INCREDIBLE EUROPEAN ADVENTURE (2007/08)

THERE is little doubt that season 2007/08 will go down as one of the most eventful in Rangers' history but for many fans it still holds a bitter-sweet taste.

It was a fantastic achievement for Rangers to reach their fourth European final. They played 18 matches in Europe which led them to the City of Manchester Stadium and the UEFA Cup final on May 14.

Sadly they lost 2-0 to Zenit St Petersburg who, ironically, were coached by former Rangers manager Dick Advocaat.

Rangers won both domestic cup competitions that season but they missed out on the League title on the final day when the sheer volume of matches caught up with them.

Overall it was incredible that a club in some disarray only 18 months earlier could recover in such a fashion.

Smith said: "Success can bring you problems. We knew that qualifying for the Champions League was a very big thing from a financial point of view but we also knew it would mean a lot of games in the first half of the campaign.

"As it turned out we continued to progress and we ended up with a fixture pile-up. I don't think there is any doubt that it had an effect on our league campaign – especially at the end of the season – but by the same token Celtic had a great finish to the season by winning their last eight games.

"We had to play four games in the last week of the season –

including the Cup final – which meant it was very difficult for our group to find the consistency needed to win the Championship but none of us would have given up the chance to play in a European final.

"The boys were fantastic throughout that season but there is no doubt the volume of games caught up with them and you can't say otherwise. In the end we lost out in the UEFA Cup final and then the league Championship so it was a big disappointment in that regard."

In the summer of 2007 Smith began to build his team. He signed Jean-Claude Darcheville, Daniel Cousin, DaMarcus Beasley, Lee McCulloch, Steven Whittaker and Steven Naismith having already secured Carlos Cuellar and Kirk Broadfoot.

Rangers had to travel to the Balkans twice to secure their place in the group phase of the Champions League and their away performances in particular gave an indication of what was to come.

Having beaten FK Zeta 2-0 at Ibrox, Rangers were organised and disciplined in Montenegro when Beasley sealed the tie with a cool finish.

There were just seconds remaining at Ibrox when Nacho Novo gave Rangers a vital 1-0 win over Red Star to take to Belgrade and in a hostile atmosphere they won through thanks to a goalless draw.

THE MEN WHO MADE HISTORY ... the Rangers team that started the UEFA Cup final at the City of Manchester Stadium on the 14th of May, 2008 - back (from left) Sasa Papac, Steven Whittaker, Brahim Hemdani, Neil Alexander, Davie Weir, Carlos Cuellar; front – Jean-Claude Darcheville, Kirk Broadfoot, Barry Ferguson, Kevin Thomson, Steve Davis.

BUILDING A NEW TEAM ... the summer of 2007 was a huge one in terms of transition as Walter Smith made major changes to the squad. He brought in Daniel Cousin from Lens (top left), Steven Naismith from Kilmarnock (bottom left) and Steven Whittaker from Hibs. Seven other newcomers met their new teammates at pre-season training in Germany (from left) Lee McCulloch, Jean-Claude Darcheville, Roy Carroll, Carlos Cuellar, Kirk Broadfoot, Alan Gow, Graeme Smith and DaMarcus Beasley.

In the group phase Rangers got off to a stunning start when they defeated Bundesliga stars Stuttgart 2-1 at Ibrox. They then surpassed that with a sensational 3-0 over Lyon in France and in a backs to the wall performance held the mighty Barca to a goal-less draw at Ibrox. They did not win another point but finished third to parachute into the UEFA Cup.

Smith said: "The Champions League can throw up some highlights and there is no doubt that our 3-0 win in Lyon was one. Lyon had dominated the French League for a number of years and they were a very strong side. We knew we would have difficulty going there but we turned in a fantastic performance.

"When Lee McCulloch got the first goal we wondered if we could maybe go on and do it and then we scored two more through Daniel Cousin and DaMarcus Beasley and it is undoubtedly one of the best European results I have ever had. It was a terrific achievement.

"We had a very good home win against Stuttgart too and also managed to hold Barcelona at home so overall when you look at the fact that we managed to qualify for the UEFA Cup from a group that featured the champions of France, Germany and Spain it was a terrific achievement."

Smith further enhanced his squad in the January window bringing Steve Davis on loan from Fulham, signing Neil Alexander from Ipswich Town and landing Christian Dailly from West Ham.

Then the story really began to unfold when they entered the UEFA Cup at the Round of 32 stage. In an incredible run, Rangers defeated Panathinaikos, Werder Bremen, Sporting Club and then won a place in the final after an electrifying penalty shoot-out win over Fiorentina in Florence with Nacho Novo scoring the clinching kick on a night no Rangers fan will ever forget.

Smith said: "Our first match in Athens was a big one because we were one down to Panathinaikos having drawn 0-0 at home and then scored late on to go through on the away goals rule.

"We then faced Bremen and we knew that would be a difficult tie but we managed to take a two-goal lead to

MUCHOS GRACIAS ... Nacho Novo celebrates his crucial strike against Red Star Belgrade on August 14, 2007 which effectively led Rangers into the Champions League and gave them the platform for a remarkable run. He was to play an even more significant role later in the campaign.

MUCHOS GRACIAS ... Nacho Novo celebrates his crucial strike against Red Star Belgrade on August 14, 2007 which effectively led Rangers into the Champions League and gave them the platform for a remarkable run. He was to play an even more significant role later in the campaign.

THE ADVENTURE BEGINS ... Walter Smith and Martin Bain arrive in Montenegro for the Champions League qualifier against FK Zeta when DaMarcus Beasley (top right) was the goal hero. Rangers were back in the Balkans in the second qualifier when Barry Ferguson and Allan McGregor celebrated after knocking out Red Star Belgrade to reach the group phase. In the opening game Walter Smith faced Armin Veh's VfB Stuttgart and Rangers recorded a terrific 2-1 win with goals from Charlie Adam (bottom left) and Jean-Claude Darcheville.

Germany and despite being under a lot of pressure and losing one goal we held on to go through.

"The Ibrox tie against the Germans was probably our best home performance of the entire European campaign and then when we went to Bremen I don't think Barcelona pinned us back as much as Thomas Schaaf's side did. Allan McGregor produced an absolutely fantastic save in the second half that kept us in it and we managed to qualify.

"I think our performance in Lisbon in the quarter-finals was a terrific one. Again we had drawn 0-0 at Ibrox but we went there and played superbly well to win 2-0 with Steven Whittaker scoring a terrific solo goal.

"The boys showed that they were gaining in confidence with each round. We knew that if we kept things tight at Ibrox we would always have a chance in the second leg because of the away goals rule and so it proved.

"We had a stalemate with Fiorentina at Ibrox and going over to Italy was always going to be very difficult and when you get to a semi-final then obviously both clubs have an eye on the final.

"There was added tension as a result but we managed to take the game into extra time and then Daniel Cousin was sent off and we thought we would be fully stretched after that and we were but we managed to remain intact and then it was penalties.

"I always feel that there is added pressure on the home team when it comes down to a shoot-out and more so Italian teams because they are always expected to do well.

"Of course Barry missed the first one so an element of doubt crept in but we got ourselves back into it and I can always remember standing in the dugout when Nacho Novo walked up and I thought it was the fourth penalty.

"Then the rest of the boys started shouting encouragement to Nacho and I said 'Is this the one that can take us through?' I had miscounted in all the drama. And when he scored it was just a fantastic moment.

"It was obviously one of the highlights of my career to take Rangers to a European final and you could tell how much it meant to everybody.

LEFT: KINGS OF LYON .... Rangers stunned French champions Olympique Lyon with a sensational 3-0 victory in the Gerland Stadium and it was Lee McCulloch who started the rout with a terrific header from a DaMarcus Beasley corner.

TAKING ON THE ELITE ... Daniel Cousin was a scorer against Lyon (top left) and no wonder Walter Smith and Kenny McDowall (top right) were smiling as they enjoyed arguably Rangers' greatest away win in Europe. The mighty Barcelona were held 0-0 at Ibrox with Nacho Novo in the thick of the action against Andres Iniesta while it was a special moment for Barry Ferguson to lead out Rangers at the Nou Camp beside Barca captain Carles Puyol even if the game was lost 2-0. Ferguson and Charlie Adam were on target in Stuttgart and Rangers boosted the squad for the UEFA Cup campaign when Steve Davis arrived on loan in January 2008.

LEFT: WUNDERBAR ... it was party time in Bremen for Rangers on March 13, 2008 when they won through to the quarter-finals of the UEFA cup, beating the Germans 2-1 on aggregate. Nacho Novo leads the celebrations with Walter Smith and his coaching staff in the background.

ABOVE: WONDERFUL TRAVELLERS ... Nacho Novo was the goal hero in Athens when Rangers knocked out Panathinaikos and he was heartily congratulated by Barry Ferguson as Walter Smith shouted instructions. In Germany Allan McGregor produced an astonishing save from Boubacar Sanogo to deny Werder Bremen and help Rangers into the last eight of the UEFA Cup.

"Of course it was a strange situation that we would then face Dick Advocaat in the final but football has a habit of throwing up things like that.

"He had formed a very good team at Zenit and it was always going to be a very difficult match for us. Equally the games had started to pile up for us ahead of the UEFA Cup final and I felt that was a bit of a disadvantage to us.

"In the final itself we didn't create an awful lot of opportunities to win. It was a tight match for a long spell and then we went behind and Zenit scored a second goal at the end.

"Like any team you are always disappointed to lose a final and we were also disappointed that we didn't acquit ourselves a little better.

"However, it was still a terrific achievement for a group which had only just been put together to get to a European final and it's something that will always stick in my mind."

IN WITH A SPORTING CHANCE ... Rangers were simply sensational in Lisbon when they knocked out Sporting with a fabulous 2-0 victory which was heartily celebrated in the Jose Alvalade Stadium. It was Jean-Claude Darcheville (bottom right) who gave them the lead and then Steven Whittaker produced a stunning solo run and finish which was voted Rangers goal of the season.

BELISSIMO ... few supporters will forget the amazing night in Florence when Rangers qualified for the UEFA Cup final on a penalty shoot-out after 210 minutes against Fiorentina had produced no goals. Nacho Novo was the man who scored the crucial penalty to spark scenes of unbridled joy but keeper Neil Alexander also played his part saving Fabio Liverani's spotkick.

There is little doubt that fixture congestion and an unwillingness of the football authorities to help ease the situation took its toll in an agonising way.

Incredibly, Rangers played 38 matches - an entire SPL season - from January 5 to May 24 and they just could not fall over the finish line in the SPL.

They actually played Celtic in the league three times in four matches, beating them at Ibrox but losing both Parkhead matches. In the final six SPL matches they only won three and Celtic took the title in the final day.

They were forced to play nine matches of huge intensity in 25 days at the end of the season including the UEFA Cup final, all of the post-split fixtures and the Scottish Cup final.

Smith said: "We were starting to draw matches and we were getting pegged back by Celtic who only had league matches to worry about. The players were getting jaded but we knew we just had to grit our teeth and try to get on with it.

"We had to play Celtic away twice in the space of nine days and we went there first after a cup tie and then after our home game with Fiorentina and we lost both to late goals.

"I am convinced that if we didn't have this fixture congestion we would have gone on and won the Championship.

"However, take nothing away from Celtic because they finished the season well and when you look at your team when you finish second you realise that we were not quite good enough when it mattered."

It was an unprecedented run of matches and there is no doubt that everyone involved will look back with some anger and resentment at the way the club was treated during this period.

There was the solace of winning both domestic cup competitions – Smith's first successes in his second spell back at the club – and it was important for the new team to show they had the ability to lift trophies. However both finals had their own dramas.

LEFT: A FABULOUS EFFORT ... Walter Smith, Neil Alexander and Steve Davis applaud the massive Rangers support at the City of Manchester stadium after the 19-game European run came to an end when Rangers just fell short against Zenit St Petersburg in the UEFA Cup final, losing 2-0.

SO CLOSE TO GLORY ... Rangers were 90 minutes away from legendary status at the UEFA Cup final when, ironically, they faced their former manager Dick Advocaat who was in charge of Zenit. He was all smiles ahead of the game with Walter Smith and it was he who was smiling at the end. Rangers, with captain Barry Ferguson pictured battling with Andrei Arshavin, had been affected by a crippling fixture list and it took its toll. But as they landed back at Glasgow Airport they could be rightly proud of an amazing European adventure.

LEFT: WINNERS AGAIN ... the first silverware since Walter Smith's return came in the League Cup final on March 16, 2008 and it was sheer drama as the game with Dundee United finished 2-2 and went to penalties.

OH BOYD! ... deadly marksman Kris Boyd was the Rangers hero at Hampden scoring twice during the match and then hitting the clinching penalty that won Rangers the cup. Allan McGregor, pictured with Boyd, made two great saves in the shootout and no wonder it was all smiles for Ally McCoist, Walter Smith and captain Barry Ferguson.

In the League Cup final on March 16 Rangers were twice behind to Dundee United both in normal time and then in extra time but Kris Boyd came to the rescue on each occasion and then scored the winning penalty in a shoot-out victory.

Remarkably, having lost out on the title at Pittodrie on Thursday May 22 Rangers returned to Glasgow, prepared on the Friday and managed to beat Queen of the South 3-2 the next day to win the Scottish Cup.

Smith said: "It was a dramatic match with Dundee United in the League Cup final because we were behind twice but came back on each occasion and then the game went to penalties and it was Kris Boyd who hit the winning kick for us.

"It's always great to win the first trophy of the season and it was the first trophy for the new group which was a good thing too.

"The Scottish Cup was a different matter because we had played at Aberdeen on the Thursday night and we were being asked to play in the Cup final on the Saturday afternoon.

"I don't think that has happened to any club in the history of Scottish football that a team has played on a Saturday then a Monday then a Thursday night in Aberdeen having to travel back from there and prepare for a cup final.

"Queen of the South had done very well to beat Aberdeen in the semi-final but with all due respect to Queens I was more worried about the fitness of my own players.

"You could see throughout the game there was a tiredness about our team but their spirit and determination managed to get us through and the 3-2 win was something we were delighted with.

"It meant we finished the season on a high by winning the Scottish Cup although overall we had mixed emotions because of being so close in the UEFA Cup and the Championship. That said it was a fantastic season for us."

RIGHT: TWO'S COMPANY ... Rangers were thrilled to win both cup competitions in Walter Smith's first full season back in charge and it was undoubtedly an indication of what was in store. Walter is pictured with his backroom team – Steve Harvey (video analysis), Ian Durrant, Ally McCoist, Pip Yeats, Kenny Scott (security chief), Kenny McDowall, Jim Stewart, Adam Owen (head of sports science) and Doctor Paul Jackson.

WHAT A FINALE ... despite a draining and intense campaign and having played in Aberdeen less than 48 hours earlier Rangers produced one last effort to lift the Scottish Cup beating Queen of the South 3-2. Again Kris Boyd was the Hampden hero scoring the opening goal and the winner with DaMarcus Beasley netting in between times.

CHAPTER EIGHT

CHAMPIONS AGAIN (2008-10)

WINNING the Championship is what playing for Rangers is all about and there was a real sense of determination that drove Walter Smith and his team in the 2008/09 season albeit after a quite disastrous start.

Smith knew there would be a hangover from the extraordinary demands of the previous campaign but he did not envisage it costing the club so dearly.

Rangers went from the incredible high of reaching a European final to the numbing low of crashing out at the first hurdle to a team they would normally deal with quite comfortably.

The 2-1 aggregate defeat by FBK Kaunas was costly as it meant no income from the Champions League when as much as £14million can be garnered from merely competing in the group phase.

However, after Rangers recovered from that shock they went on to produce a fantastic League and Cup Double and followed it up the next season by retaining the title with some ease and adding the League Cup for good measure.

These successes were achieved against a backdrop of financial difficulties, especially in the second season and that's what makes them all the more impressive.

There was doggedness and resilience about the group of players that Smith had assembled and they deserved their rewards.

He said: "When you play nearly 70 games a season you know you are going to have a problem at the start of the next season. You just can't play that amount of games for it not to have an effect.

"Our pre-season games had been flat. I remember a match at Raith Rovers in particular when we just could not get ourselves up for the game at all and somehow managed to win 2-1.

"I think we all knew then we were going to have a problem. We went over to Kaunas and we were holding on at 1-1 which would have taken us through on the away goals rule. I just felt if we could get through that tie then we would have time to regroup for the next one – but we didn't do so.

"So from the high of our great European run the previous season we suffered the low of being knocked out before our season had really started.

"It was hard to take but I realised that it was not unexpected and we were then in a situation where our season was going to be quite different from the one before and we got stronger and stronger as the season went on.

"We managed to go on and win the Championship which we were thrilled to do. We were not affected by extra matches and we had a good strength and vitality about our squad."

Before the Kaunas debacle Rangers had managed to recruit Kyle Lafferty and Kenny Miller which was a bold move given that even though he had played for Rangers before, he had played a season for Gordon Strachan's Celtic. There were some fans who were not happy.

More pressingly he was forced into selling Carlos Cuellar to Aston Villa after the Spanish defender invoked a clause in his contract and it wasn't until after Rangers were out of Europe that he found a replacement in Madjid Bougherra and was able to bolster the squad with the signings of Pedro Mendes,

PRIZE GUYS ... the joy on the faces of Kenny McDowall, Walter Smith and Ally McCoist is there for all to see after the fantastic title triumph at Tannadice in May 2009.

Maurice Edu and the full-time capture of Steve Davis from Fulham.

Smith said: "You don't always want to continually change your players but in some instances you have little choice and that was the case with Carlos Cuellar who, like many Spanish players, had a clause in his contract where he could leave; the figure being 8 million Euros.

"Aston Villa offered the money and regretfully we had to let him go. We managed to get Madjid Bougherra to come in and he proved to be an excellent replacement.

"We also managed to get Kenny Miller in and of course he was one that was not quite accepted by everyone at our club because of his spell at Celtic. However, he had played well for me when I was Scotland manager and I felt he would be a good player for Rangers.

"Sometimes you have to make decisions that don't please some people – that's the life of a manager – but I think I got this one right because over the period he was an excellent player for Rangers."

Miller and Mendes certainly had the fans in raptures on August 31, 2008 when Rangers went to Parkhead and demolished Celtic 4-2 with Miller striking a double to immediately ingratiate himself with his detractors and Mendes producing a stunning drive from the edge of the box.

Rangers then went on an unbeaten run until the end of December but they lost 1-0 to Celtic at Ibrox to fall seven points behind their rivals and the pressure was on. They got it down to two points by February and when Steve Davis scored a great winner in the final Old Firm game of the season Rangers had a two point cushion of their own.

The drama, however, was not over. The Light Blues promptly drew 1-1 with Hibs and that put Celtic back on top on goal difference with two matches to play. The pressure was intense and Rangers defeated Aberdeen 2-1 at Ibrox and then saw Celtic held 0-0 by Hibs.

And so the helicopter was called again but unlike 2005

THE NEW BOYS ... Walter Smith bolstered his squad for the 2008/09 campaign by bringing some top players. Kenny Miller returned to the club while £3.5million was spent to land Kyle Lafferty from Burnley. Portuguese playmaker Pedro Mendes was signed from Portsmouth, Maurice Edu came from Major League Soccer outfit Toronto, Steve Davis was signed permanently from Fulham and Madjid Bougherra arrived from Charlton.

GAMES THAT WON THE TITLE ... Maurice Edu is mobbed by his teammates (top left) after a vital clinching goal in a 3-2 win over Hibs while Kenny Miller (centre) and Pedro Mendes were goal heroes in the stunning 4-2 victory over Celtic in August 2008 and Steve Davis was a derby star in the 1-0 Old Firm win in May 2009.

Rangers had their destiny in their own hands and promptly thumped Dundee United 3-0 at Tannadice with goals from Kyle Lafferty, Pedro Mendes and Kris Boyd. The title was back.

Smith said: "It was a huge moment. I know the demands at Rangers and having just missed out on the title the year before I knew we were under pressure to win it in that season.

"Whether you get to European finals or win domestic cups the onus is always on you to win the Championship and there was a great determination among our group to do so.

"Once you get towards that winning position it becomes like a cup tie and it felt that way when we went to Tannadice where, of course, I had spent a lot of time and where I had also had a lot of successes before.

"We had won nine in a row there so to go back there and win the title again was very special. You always worry about a game like that because there is so much tension but the boys were excellent right from the start of the game and thoroughly deserved their win.

"When we got back to Ibrox there were 30,000 there and it was fantastic. Rangers and Celtic never have the chance to go round the city in an open-top bus so it was great to see so many fans back at the stadium to greet the team."

Rangers had lost out to Celtic in the League Cup final in extra time in March but they finished the season with more silverware when Nacho Novo's outrageous volley dipped under the Falkirk crossbar.

Smith said: "I think we were in a situation where we had placed all of our emphasis on winning the league campaign and when we achieved that I knew that it would be a bit difficult to motivate everyone again in the Scottish Cup final.

"We didn't play at our best and Falkirk played very well in the game but Nacho got us one of his special goals and it won us the Cup. Of course it was terrific to win another trophy."

It was a special season but it had been tinged with

LEFT: LOVELY BUBBLY ... the delirious Rangers players celebrate in style in the dressing room at Tannadice after their magnificent final day title triumph in 2009.

WE ARE THE CHAMPIONS ... Kris Boyd (top left) and Pedro Mendes (top right) were goal heroes in the 3-0 win over Dundee United that clinched the title and meant that the helicopter headed for Tayside. Walter Smith celebrated the magnificent achievement with captain Barry Ferguson and his backroom staff.

MAKE MINE A DOUBLE ... Rangers clinched the League and Cup Double when they defeated Falkirk in the Scottish Cup final in May 2009 when Nacho Novo scored a spectacular winning goal. Caring grandfather Walter allowed his granddaughter Jessica to share the moment with him.

LEFT: IT AIN'T WHAT EDU, IT'S THE WAY THAT EDU IT ...

Kenny Miller celebrates with Maurice Edu after his dramatic winner against Celtic on February 28, 2010.

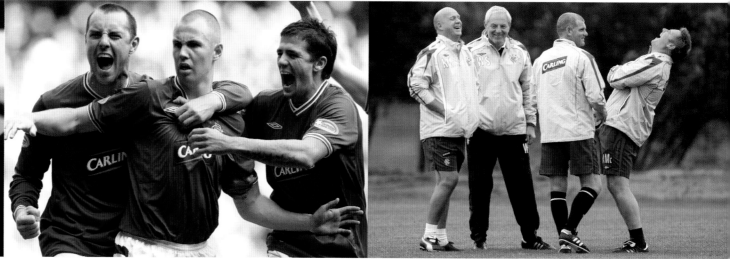

ABOVE: FUN AND GAMES ...

Walter Smith got into in a bit of trouble at Rugby Park when he was sent to the stand by referee Steve Conroy during a goalless draw on September 19, 2009 but that was all forgotten when Kenny Miller scored twice against Celtic a month later and, of course, there was always room for a laugh on the training ground.

controversy in late March when captain Barry Ferguson and goalkeeper Allan McGregor were at the centre of a scandal when they – and other Scotland players – sat up drinking to the early hours at Cameron House Hotel.

Both players then exacerbated the situation when they made rude gestures to press photographers and cameramen when sitting on the Hampden bench ahead of the World Cup qualifying tie with the Faroes. Smith had to act, although he was far from pleased with the SFA's handling of the affair.

He suspended the pair and fined them two weeks' wages. It was at this point that the SFA decided to ban them from representing Scotland again and subsequently changed their minds the following season.

McGregor did not play again that season but was forgiven and went on to reclaim his No1 slot while Ferguson played in the final three games of the season before moving to Birmingham that summer.

LEFT: **IT'S MILLER TIME ...** it was simply stunning when Kenny Miller won the League Cup for Rangers on March 2010 when Rangers were down to nine men against St Mirren.

WALT A VICTORY ... manager Smith can't hide his emotions after an unbelievable victory at Hampden against all of the odds.

Smith said: "It's like every problem you encounter in management, I could have done without it. However, as a manager when things happen you have to be decisive. You have to show you are taking control of the situation.

"Smaller things happen every other week, whether it's taking action against players or leaving players out and you make decisions but you do this in the relative privacy of your own club. Clearly this was a very public thing.

"It meant the players missing a number of games which, when you are going for a Championship, was not an easy decision to make but I felt from the club's point of view it was the only thing we could do.

"Barry was the captain of both Rangers and Scotland and Allan had been in terrific form in goal for us. You don't want to lose players of that quality but the decision had to be made and we had to live with the consequences.

"Fortunately there were no real consequences for us and the two players were integrated back into the squad later in the season.

"But I still feel it all could have been avoided and it was disappointing that it was left to us to take the action that we did."

It had been Smith's intention to hand over the reins to Ally McCoist in the summer of 2009 but he was convinced to remain and he brought more glories to savour.

He said: "From the outset I was coming back to Rangers for a short period with the idea being to hand over to Alastair. At the end of the 2008/09 season I was thinking that this would be done.

"However, I was convinced by my boys to change my mind.

They came to me and said that they were more than delighted for me to carry on. They said they were not in any hurry to take over so I agreed to remain."

Remarkably, despite being unable to bring in any players from January 2009 until the summer of 2010 Rangers won the championship for the second successive season with some ease.

The start to the season was far from convincing. Three goalless draws in succession in September against Motherwell, Kilmarnock and Aberdeen meant Rangers went into the first Old Firm game of the season on October 4 four points behind Celtic.

However, it was another joyous day for Kenny Miller in particular as he scored twice in a 2-1 win at Ibrox which undoubtedly kick-started the team once more. Over the winter months Rangers were devastating scoring 23 goals in five consecutive wins.

When Lee McCulloch equalised at Parkhead on January 2 to give Rangers a 1-1 draw they were seven points ahead of Celtic, who had played a game fewer, and their rivals never got close to them again.

Indeed, Mo Edu's last-gasp winner in the February 28 Old Firm game at Ibrox effectively ended Celtic's challenge.

They had been consistent for most of the campaign whereas Celtic under Tony Mowbray were sporadic and he paid for that with his job before the season was over.

Rangers clinched the crown at Easter Road on April 25 when Lafferty scored the only goal to spark fantastic celebrations both in Edinburgh and again back at Ibrox.

The European campaign was a poor one with only two draws

SAVOURING THE MOMENT ... the triumphant Rangers squad celebrate their remarkable League Cup success back at Ibrox in the home dressing room.

from the six Champions League group games and that hurt Smith and his players. There was also carelessness in the Scottish Cup when Rangers frittered away a 3-1 lead over Dundee United in the quarter-final and then lost the replay at Tannadice.

However, the League Cup was something quite extraordinary when Rangers had both Kevin Thomson and Danny Wilson sent off and yet prevailed against St Mirren in the March 21 final.

Smith said: "People say that we won the Championship comfortably in 2010 but we never looked at it like that. In actual fact when you have more of a points gap then as a manager you are more inclined to have nerves.

"If everything is tight then you know you have to go out and win every game whereas if you have a bit of a cushion then it brings its own problems.

"We went to Easter Road knowing that even if we lost that game we would still have more opportunities to win the title but we wanted to do it that day.

"I was delighted that the team managed to win on that day. Winning back to back Championships is a very big thing.

"I have to admit that our drive and focus was winning the Championship and I think that had a bearing going into the League Cup final.

"St Mirren were the better side in the first half of the game and I had to have a bit of a managerial rant at half-time, which I hadn't had to do very often in my second spell.

"I don't know if that led to the circumstances where there was an extra edge to the players but Kevin Thomson was sent off and then we had Danny Wilson sent off too.

"We were suddenly in circumstances that few if any teams have been in – down to nine men, sitting at 0-0 and not playing at their best.

"But what a reaction we got. We actually played better with nine men than we did with 11 and it is sometimes natural for players to do that because they know they have to do something special.

"Then Steven Naismith burst down the right crossed into middle and Kenny Miller scored with a header. Suddenly we were in the lead and the trick was trying to hold onto it. When the final whistle went I think we all felt it so much. It was a remarkable achievement by everyone to handle the circumstances of that game."

It had been a fantastic campaign again and this time Smith made it clear to everyone – the next season was to be his last and what a season it turned out to be.

JUST CHAMPION ... it was another title-winning moment for Walter Smith when Rangers defeated Hibs at Easter Road on April 25 and he lapped it up in front of the joyous fans.

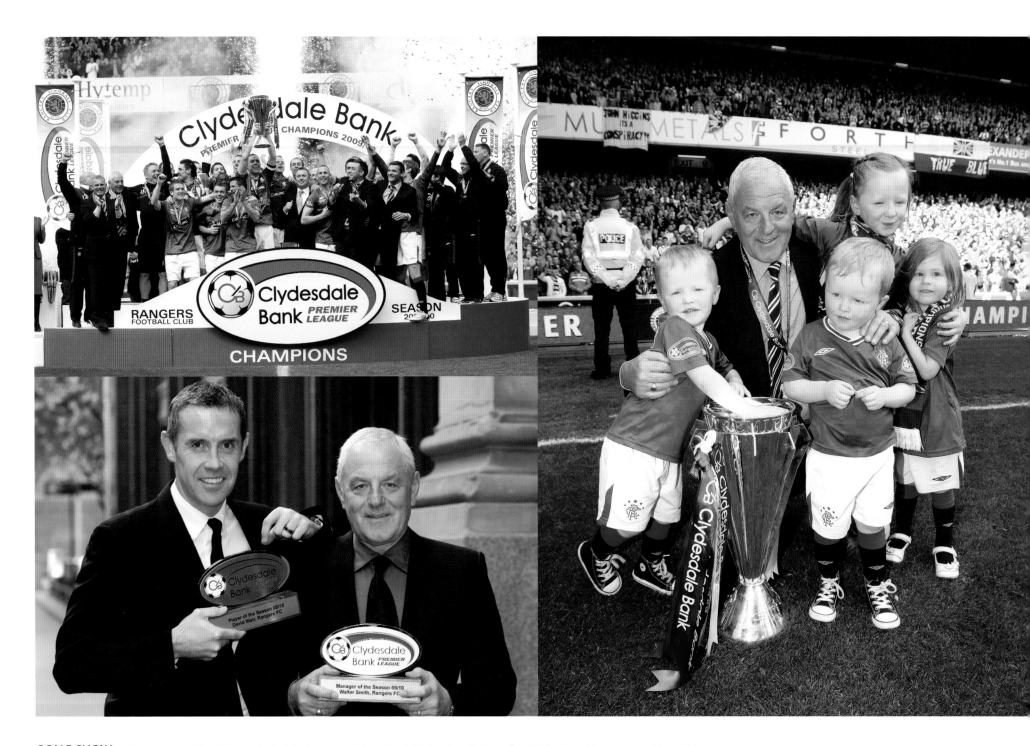

GONG SHOW ... Rangers received the SPL trophy in their final league match on May 9, 2010 against Motherwell and Walter shared the moment with grandsons Adam and Jack, grand-daughter Jessica and Ian Durrant's daughter Carys. He and Davie Weir were voted Manager and Player of the Year by SPL sponsors Clydesdale Bank.

IT'S A DEAL ... Walter and Ally McCoist both signed new contracts with chief executive Martin Bain on May 25 after an exhilarating campaign.

CHAPTER NINE

OUT IN A BLAZE OF GLORY
(2010/11)

THE INCREDIBLE scenes at Rugby Park on May 15, 2011 were the perfect way for Walter Smith to bow out as Rangers manager when the Light Blues clinched three titles in a row in emphatic fashion.

For the fifth time in eight seasons the SPL Championship race had gone to the final day. Rangers held a one-point lead over Celtic who were facing Motherwell at home and ready to take advantage of any Rangers slip at Kilmarnock.

The stakes were huge and, for the third time, the SPL hired a helicopter to deliver the trophy to the destination of the winners. However, any trepidation anyone had was blown away inside seven minutes when Smith's side scored three times inside the first seven minutes of their match making Celtic's 4-0 win irrelevant.

In the end Rangers won 5-1 to claim the Championship for the 54th time in their history and give their legendary manager his 21st major honour in two extraordinary spells as boss.

The scenes back at Ibrox were equally joyous as close to 40,000 ecstatic fans poured into the ground to salute the great man, his staff and his players. It was quite simply the perfect send-off.

Outwith the trophy-laden nine in a row period it was the first time Rangers had won three successive crowns since the 1930s which is another indication of the magnificent achievement of Walter Smith and his team. He ended it all in style, with dignity and as a winner.

He said of the final day triumph: "Sometimes when you are coming to the end and everyone knows you are leaving the focus goes on you and that's unfair on the rest of the boys.

"I was worried that it would be about me rather than all of us but the boys handled that aspect of it the way they have handled all of the problems we have encountered over the past few years – extremely well.

"It was a fantastic way to go out. We had a lot of difficulties but we overcame them and if ever a group of players deserved to win the Championship it was them.

"You just have to look to a couple of years ago when all of them were up for sale and yet they committed themselves to the club which was a fantastic thing."

It was an epic campaign in so many ways because both Kevin Thomson and Danny Wilson were sold while fans' favourite Nacho Novo moved on and Kenny Miller left for Bursaspor in the middle of it.

There were serious injuries to £4million signing Nikica Jelavic, Lee McCulloch and Stevie Naismith while Kirk Broadfoot missed virtually all of the campaign. And yet Rangers not only prevailed but defeated Celtic in a terrific League Cup final and restored the credibility on the European stage.

There were massive wins at massive times when Jelavic

WALT A SEND-OFF ... the Rangers fans gave Smith a fantastic reception at his final home match against Dundee United on May 10, 2011.

JEL OF A PLAYER ... Walter spent £4million on Croatian star Nikica Jelavic and he was a key man in a fantastic final season.

ABOVE, LEFT AND CENTRE: LOANS WITH INTEREST ... Vladimir Weiss and Richard Foster were brought in on loan from Manchester City and Aberdeen and played important roles in a terrific campaign.

ABOVE, RIGHT: A PORTRAIT OF YOU ... captain Davie Weir hands over a special painting of Walter Smith that the players had bought at auction at the Rangers Charity Ball.

grabbed crucial winning goals at Pittodrie both in September and April – the former coming after Rangers had gone two goals down. Naismith hit a last-minute winner at Tynecastle on October 2 while loan star Vladimir Weiss forced Tim Clancy to deflect the ball into his own net for an absolutely crucial win over Kilmarnock on April 13.

Allan McGregor played his part with a superb penalty save from Georgios Samaras in the final Old Firm game of the season on April 24 which ensured a goalless draw which was to prove pivotal in Rangers' success.

It was an old friend in Terry Butcher who aided Rangers in their quest for three in a row when his Inverness side defeated Celtic with four games to go and from that moment it was in Rangers' hands to win.

The Champions League was special too as Smith was given the chance to lead his side against his old friend Sir Alex Ferguson when Rangers were drawn in a group that featured Manchester United, Valencia and Bursaspor.

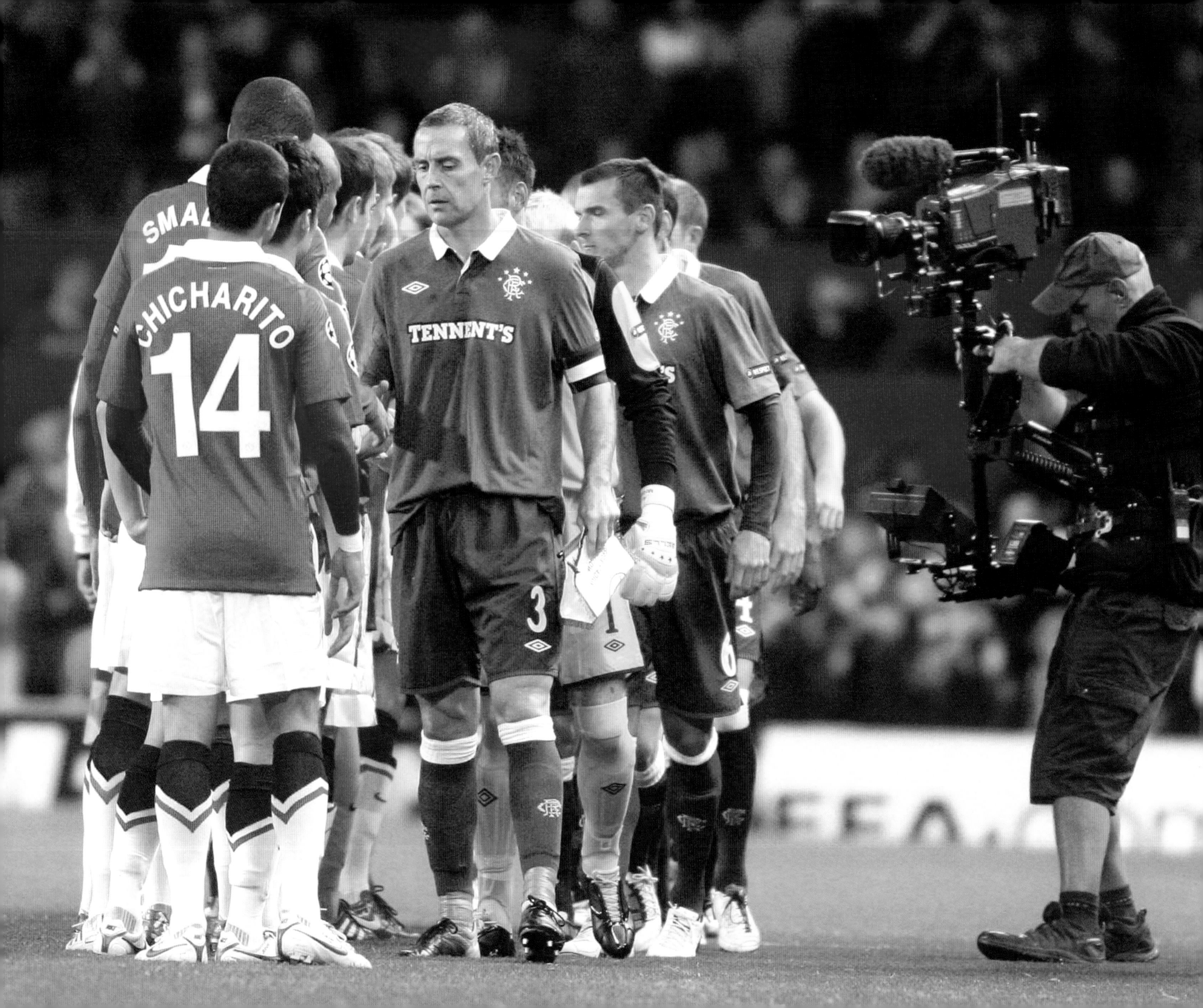
CHICHARITO
14
TENNENT'S
3

Creditably they held the mighty Red Devils on their own patch, they were desperately unfortunate to only draw 1-1 at Ibrox with the Spaniards and they secured third place in the group by beating the Turks at home and drawing 1-1 in Bursa.

That allowed them to parachute into the Europa League and again they performed with great credit knocking out Sporting in Lisbon thanks to a last-gasp goal from Maurice Edu but just fell short against PSV Eindhoven in the last 16, losing 1-0 at Ibrox.

There was certainly no hangover from the European exit because Rangers produced a performance of great flair, strength and purpose to defeat Celtic in extra time in the League Cup final.

The Light Blues were without a win against Celtic in four matches but they turned on the style at Hampden and – amazingly – both of their goals hit the same post before going into the net.

It was Steve Davis who gave them the lead when he moved forward and hit a left foot shot past the giant frame of Fraser Forster which hit the inside of the right hand post. Joe Ledley found an equaliser for Celtic and the match went to extra time.

Suddenly Weiss surprised Celtic with a quick free kick which sent Jelavic racing through the middle and he slipped the ball past the Celtic keeper. It hit the inside of the right post, spun at least a yard in front of the line and then back into the net at the other side.

Smith said: "That was a fantastic occasion. We went to Hampden for the win and I think we deserved it. My team was excellent that day and everyone played exceptionally well.

"I was delighted for every one of the players because they had taken some criticism in the previous matches with Celtic. It was always going to be a tight one but I'm glad we came out on top because it would have been tough on the players if they hadn't.

"We created more chances and had far more opportunities to score and we probably should have won the game in 90 minutes so there were concerns

LEFT: FIELD OF DREAMS ... Davie Weir led out Rangers at Old Trafford in the Champions League where Rangers fought out a creditable goalless draw with Manchester United.

ABOVE: RESTORING PRIDE ... Rangers made a decent effort in the Champions League when Stevie Naismith (top left) scored the winner against Bursaspor and Mo Edu was on target – albeit at both ends – in the 1-1 draw with Valencia. Steven Whittaker relished coming up against Ryan Giggs and Walter met an old friend in Valencia in Jocky Bjorklund who works for local radio. It was a joyous night in Lisbon when El-Hadji Diouf scored and Mo Edu sealed qualification late on.

KEY MOMENTS OF THE CAMPAIGN ... Allan McGregor's penalty save from Georgios Samaras on April 24 was undoubtedly pivotal for Rangers. Kenny Miller maintained his remarkable record against Celtic with another double on October 24, 2010 while Stevie Naismith's late strike at Tynecastle earlier that month was crucial. Sasa Papac and Vladimir Weiss celebrate the 2-1 win over Kilmarnock and Kyle Lafferty and Nikica Jelavic jump for joy at Pittodrie.

FOLLOWING THE MASTER ... it was officially announced in February 2011 that Ally McCoist was to take over from Walter Smith at the end of the season.

DEADLINE DEALS ... young defender Kyle Bartley and sometimes explosive attacker El-Hadji Diouf joined Rangers on loan in the January window and undoubtedly played their parts in a fabulous season.

that things could go wrong in extra time because Celtic had dangerous forwards who were capable of getting a goal out of nothing.

"However, we found a winning goal. It did take a long time to cross the line and even then, I thought a Celtic player had managed to get back to it and keep it out. Thankfully that wasn't the case though and we managed to get a really big victory which we all enjoyed."

The Hampden triumph was undoubtedly the catalyst for Rangers to go on and win the Championship. They won nine and drew one of their remaining 10 fixtures which is undoubtedly impressive form.

Of course there were two other major moments in the campaign with Ally McCoist officially announced on February 22 as the man to replace Walter Smith and then just nine days before the end of the season the club changed hands.

After 23 incredible years as Rangers owner Sir David Murray concluded a deal with Craig Whyte to sell the club so the finale to the 2010/11 season was the end of an era in more ways than one.

Smith and Murray enjoyed some remarkable times together at Rangers, arguably in the most successful period in Rangers' history, and both men hope new glories are lying in wait for McCoist under the stewardship of Whyte.

In typically modest fashion Smith paid tribute to those around as he offered his final thoughts on his remarkable times with Rangers

He said: "I must admit when I go back to the start you think about all of the great moments you have.

"People ask me what was the best but I can't separate them. I'm just delighted to have been a successful Rangers manager. There were great Rangers managers before me who brought great successes to the club and I'm just pleased and feel very fortunate that I have been able to follow them.

"To become Rangers manager was the biggest thing in my career and I feel honoured that I was given the

ARMS WIDE OPEN ... Walter Smith celebrates the dramatic League Cup final triumph over Celtic which proved to be a real catalyst in the race for the flag.

HAMPDEN HEROES ... Steve Davis and Nikica Jelavic got the goals in the 2-1 win over Celtic which sparked fantastic scenes at the national stadium and then back at Ibrox.

A SALUTE TO A LEGEND ... the Rangers fans showed their appreciation for Walter at his final home match in charge on May 10 with a terrific ovation which he enjoyed with grandchildren Jessica, Adam and Jack despite the torrential rain!

chance not once but twice.

"I am also fortunate that I have had some great people around me in both periods at Rangers in terms of staff and players. No manager can succeed without that regardless of whatever talents he may have.

"People talk about 'grooming' Ally McCoist but that's not the case because I knew the talents that he had. When I took the Scotland job and asked him to join me I knew what his qualities were.

"Many people see the jovial character and the bubbly personality – and he has that – but he has a hard edge to him and a desire to be successful at whatever he does. I always felt that he had managerial qualities and hopefully with a bit of help from everyone at Rangers he will be successful.

"I will be back as a supporter. I won't be back that often initially because when you make a break like I am doing then I feel it is better to stay away. However, I will be watching with interest.

"I have been fortunate that my boys were brilliant for me – Alastair, Kenny McDowall, Ian Durrant, Jim Stewart, Paul Jackson and Pip Yeats and all of the backroom team.

"I sincerely hope that they all give the same backing to Alastair and they can all continue to bring a great level of success to Rangers.

"There will be parts of the job I will miss, particularly the camaraderie of your colleagues. They made coming to work a pleasure.

"The players were great to work with. I can count on one hand the number of times I had to step in and lift training because the boys always worked hard.

"They always tried to do their best on the field and their commitment could not be faulted. Of course we had some disappointments along the way but they always attempted to bring success to the club.

"So I will miss the pleasure of winning matches and winning competitions.

"Overall I feel fortunate. Rangers is a fantastic club."

KILLIE HIGHS... Stevie Naismith, Kyle Lafferty and a squashed Nikica Jelavic got the goals in the thumping 5-1 win over Kilmarnock that won the title to spark wild celebrations among the Rangers fans especially when Davie Weir and Walter lifted the trophy.

WALTER SMITH'S RANGERS RECORDS

LEAGUE

	P	W	D	L	F	A	PTS	
1990-91	4	3	0	1	4	3	6	W*
1991-92	44	33	6	5	101	31	72	W*
1992-93	44	33	7	4	97	35	73	W*
1993-94	44	22	14	8	74	41	58	W*
1994-95	36	20	9	7	60	35	69	W
1995-96	36	27	6	3	85	25	87	W
1996-97	36	25	5	6	85	33	80	W
1997-98	36	21	9	6	76	38	72	2nd
2006-07	15	10	3	2	26	10	33	2nd
2007-08	38	27	5	6	84	33	86	2nd
2008-09	38	26	8	4	77	28	86	W
2009-10	38	26	9	3	82	28	87	W
2010-11	38	30	3	5	88	29	93	W
TOTAL	447	303	84	60	939	369	902	

*2 points for a win

EUROPEAN

		P	W	D	L	F	A	
1991-92	European Cup	2	1	0	1	2	2	R1
1992-93	European Cup	10	6	4	0	14	7	CL Gp (2nd)
1993-94	European Cup	2	1	0	1	4	4	R1
1994-95	European Cup	2	0	0	2	0	3	prelim
1995-96	European Cup	8	1	4	3	7	14	CL Gp (4th)
1996-97	European Cup	8	3	0	5	15	16	CL Gp (4th)
1997-98	European Cup	4	2	1	1	12	4	qual
1997-98	UEFA Cup	2	0	0	2	2	4	R1
2006-07	UEFA Cup	4	1	1	2	6	4	last 16
2007-08	European Cup	10	5	2	3	11	8	CL Gp (3rd)
2007-08	UEFA Cup	9	2	5	2	5	4	F
2008-09	European Cup	2	0	1	1	1	2	qual
2009-10	European Cup	6	0	2	4	4	13	CL Gp (4th)
2010-11	European Cup	6	1	3	2	3	6	CL Gp (3rd)
2010-11	UEFA Cup	4	0	3	1	3	4	last 16
	TOTAL	79	23	26	30	89	95	

SCOTTISH CUP

	P	W	D	L	F	A	
1991-92	5	5	0	0	9	2	W
1992-93	5	5	0	0	11	2	W
1993-94	6	4	1	1	14	3	F
1994-95	2	1	0	1	5	5	R4
1995-96	5	5	0	0	24	4	W
1996-97	3	2	0	1	5	2	QF
1997-98	7	4	2	1	12	7	F
2007-08	7	5	2	0	14	4	W
2008-09	5	5	0	0	15	1	W
2009-10	6	2	3	1	9	7	QF
2010-11	3	1	1	1	5	3	R5
TOTAL	54	39	9	6	123	40	

LEAGUE CUP

	P	W	D	L	F	A	
1991-92	4	3	0	1	9	1	SF
1992-93	5	5	0	0	18	4	W
1993-94	5	5	0	0	8	2	W
1994-95	2	1	0	1	7	3	R3
1995-96	4	3	0	1	8	4	SF
1996-97	5	5	0	0	20	5	W
1997-98	3	2	0	1	5	2	QF
2007-08	4	4	0	0	10	3	W
2008-09	4	3	0	1	7	3	F
2009-10	4	4	0	0	8	2	W
2010-11	4	4	0	0	13	4	W
TOTAL	44	39	0	5	113	33	

OVERALL

	P	W	D	L	F	A
Premier League	447	303	84	60	939	369
Scottish Cup	54	39	9	6	123	40
League Cup	44	39	0	5	113	33
European Cup	60	20	17	23	73	79
UEFA Cup	19	3	9	7	16	16
TOTAL	624	404	119	101	1264	537

WALTER
THANK YOU FOR THE MEMORIES

Victor Adair	Ralph Beattie	Martin Campbell	John Sinclair Currie	Marc Finnigan
Peter Adamson	Ross Beattie	Stanley Gordon Campbell	Ellen Cuthbert	Catherine C Fisher
Scott Adamson	Craig Bell	Jum Cannie	David Dale	Scott Fitzpatrick
Matthew Aird	Philip Bell	David Cargill	Louisa Dale	Cammy Fleming
Margaret Aitken	William Bellshaw	Julie Carson	Craig Davidson	Johnny Fleming
Alex Aitken	John Bennett	W Carswell	Charlene Davis	Scott Fletcher
David Alexander	Lee William Bennett	Christopher Cartwright	Stewart Daye	Clark Fortune
David Alexander	Bob Beveridge	Iain Cathcart	Alex Dayer	Billy Fraser
Kevin Alexander	Dave Biggans	Heather Charnley	Douglas Deans	Bob Fraser
Marc Alexander	Mark Billingham	Craig Chirrey	Brian Tom Dempsey	Derek Fraser
David Allan	Suzi Blackburn	Ian Chirrey	Ian T Denholm	Douglas Penman Fraser
James Allan	Jim Blues	Steven Clanachan	John Devine	George French
James Stewart Allan	Ross Blyth	Robert Clark	Jim Dewar	Ian Fyfe Frew
Jordan Allan	Allan Booth	William Clelland	Ross Dewar	Patrick Friel
Robin Allan	Roger Bovell	Brian Clements	Mark John Dickie	Billy Fulton
David Anderson	Angus & Mary Brewer	Jim Clifford	Robert Dickie	Thomas Fulton
Ian S Anderson	Rana & Cole Brewer	James Clydesdale	William Dickie	Derek Fulton
Robert Anderson	George Brown	Alex & Nev Cohen	Andrew Dickson	Robert Galbraith
Ruairidh Anderson	James Brown	William Coid	Kev Dickson	Robert Gallacher
Stewart Anderson	Mary Ann Brown	Sara Colley	Bill Donaldson	Sandy Galletly
John Andrews	David Bruce	Gary Connor	James Cordiner Donaldson IV	David Galloway
Adrian Angus	Gordon M Bruce	Mike Conway	Vic Donati	Aaron Gardiner
Linda Annett	David Bryant	Terence R Cook	Cameron Dougherty	David Gebbie
Jeffrey Annette	James Buchanan	David Cooper	Agnes Douglas	Peter George
Jim Annette	Stewart B Buchanan	Ryan Frederick Cooper	Robert Douglas	David V Gibb
Jonathan Annette	Stuart Buchanan	Lee Coutts	Jonathan Drain	Edward Gibson
Mrs Mary Archbold	Louisa Buchanan	Gordon Cowan	Derrick Duff	Francis Gilchrist
Gary Armstrong	Mary Burns	Barry Cox	Scott Duffy	John Gilday
Mark Armstrong	William Burrell	John L Coyle	Robert Duncan	James Gillan
Roger Arnold	David Burrill	Douglas Craig	Stewart Dunn	Graham Gilmour
Paige Spence Ashley	Michael Burton	Douglas Craig	Jennifer Easton	John Girvan
Iain Auld	George Bustard	Alison S Crawford	Glen Edgar	Allan Gleeson
John W Bacon	Martin Gilmartin Cairns	John Creedican	John Muir Edwards	William Mochrie Glendinning
Mr J K Bagnall	Sharon Cairns	Jim Creighton	Mark Elliot	Dougie Gordon
James Bain	Andrew S Calder	Jean Cresswell	Spencer Evans	Dr. Benjamin D. Goss
Richard Baird	David Calder	Dave Crompton	William Eyre	Alex Gourlay
Peter & Joan Ball	James Calder	Stuart Cruickshank	Walter Farmer	Jacqueline Gourlay
Gordon Bannister	Marion Cameron	Colin Cumming	Sam Fenn	James M Gourlay
Brian Douglas Barclay	Glenn Campbell	Des Currens	Alan Ferguson	Louise Gourlay
Stewart Barton	Jim Campbell	Alexander Currie	Andrew Fernie	Ralph Gourlay

Sandra Gourlay
Stuart Govan
Eddie Graham
William Graham
Denis Grant
David Gray
Iain Gray
Thomas Greenfield
Thomas Greenfield
Peter Grierson
Andrew Hadden
Steven Haddow
Niklas Haglund
Callum Haining
Colin Hall
Andrew Hannah
Jim Hannah
Robert Rowland Hannah
Andrew Hannah
Cameron Hannah
Scott Hannah
Marc Harper
Robert Harper
Walter McCulloch Harris
Daniel Hart
Robert Hart
Alan Harvey
Keith Hawley
Andy Hay
Scott Heaney
David Heggie
William Henderson
Willie Henderson
Lee Herd
Lindsay Herron
Robert Hill
Steven Hill
Andrew Holmes
Bill Holmes
Graeme Horvath
Gary Hosie
Steven Hotson
Harry Houston
Natalie Houston

Andrew Robert Hunter
Charles William Wiotti Hunter
David Archibald Hunter
James Hunter
Tam Hunter
Rab Hutton
Graham Hyde
William Hynds
Ross Inglis
Brian Philip Innes
Gordon Harry Irving
Alistair McKinnon Jack
Gary Charles Jackson
Bobby Jamieson
John Jamieson
John Jamison
Sammie Jayne
Michael Jepson
Allan Johnstone
Gordon Johnstone
Melvyn Johnstone
James Jones
Mick Jones
Hilary Kane
William Kay & Cindy Kay
Lisa Keir
Billy Kelman
James Kennedy
John Kennedy
David Kerr
Eddie Kerr
Samuel Kerr
Stephen Kerr
Ross Kikland
Stuart Kilty
Robert Knape
James Kurth
Will Laing
William J Lamont
Andrew Lang
Stuart Langan
Donnie Lawson
Jim Leishman

Rob Letham
Samuel James Liddell
Allan Linton
Danny Litster
Thomas Little
Joseph Livingstone
William Loach
Cameron Lockhart
Leigh Lockhart
Rhonda Logan
James Logue
Douglas Loudon
Baillie Loyal
Roddy Lumsden
Billy Lyall
Trevor Lyness
Billy Lynn
Roderick MacAffer
Matthew MacCallum
Angus MacCuish
Callum MacCuish
Gordon Macdiarmid
Neil MacIsaac MacDonald
Allan Macdonald & Family
Duncan Macfarlane
Alastair MacGregor
Thomas Mackay
Angus Murdo Mackenzie
Scott MacKenzie
Charlie MacKinnon
Murdo MacKinnon
Laura Maclean
James MacLennan
John N Macleod
Norrie MacLeod
Lachlan MacNeil
Neil Magill
Joseph Mair
Paul Manning
Roberto Manservisi
Robert M Manson
Gary Maplesden
Wilfred Marshall
Fiona Martin

David Martin
Colin Massie
Colin Mathers
Jack Mathieson
Phil & Suzanne Mayes
Greig McAfee
Jenny McAleese
Gordon McAllister
Stewart McAllister
Peter McArdle
Gordon McAteer
Steven McCahon
Paul McCann
David McClean
Mark McClory
James McClung
Archie McCluskey
Drew McComb
Gordon McComb
Alexander McCombie
John McConnachie
Derek McCracken
Stephen McCrimmon
Sarah McCullagh
John McCutcheon
"Alistair, Karl & Kurt" McDonald
Graeme McDonald
Mary Alice McDougall
John McElroy
Pauline McEwan
John McFarlane
Kirk McFarlane
Lyndsey McFarlane
William McFarlane
Richard McFetridge
Alan McGarvie
Thomas McGee
Laura McGeoch
Alexander McGhee
Janet McGillivray
Archie McGilvary
Hugh McGinnigle
Dougie McGlashan

James McGraw
Elizabeth A McGregor
Robert Cocker McGregor
Stephen McGrew
Roslyn McGuinness
John McGuire
Duncan McInnes
Brian P McIntosh
Derek McIntosh
Gordon McIntosh
Lynn McIntosh
Norman J McIntosh
Scott McIntosh
Irene Mckechnie
Peter Mckechnie
Paul McKee
John Mckee Snr
Alexander McKeeman
Gordon Thomas McKenzie
Donald McKerrell
Jack McKillop
John McKinnon
Robert McKnight
Sam McLaren
Glen McLean
George McLeod
William Andrew McMahon
Anthony McManus
Gordon Connor McMillan
Sam McMillan
Angus Alexander McMurchy
Bruce McMurchy
Peter McDonald McNab
Fraser Royal McNaught
Gary McNeil
Grant McNeil
Christopher McNicol
Noel McNulty
Robert McPhee
Malky McPherson
Alan McPhillie
Mary McVey
Samuel McVey
Marc McWilliam